endure

A Memoir of Grief, Resilience, and Love

Kelly McCoy

COLLECTIVE

copyright

praise for endure

"Kelly, your writing touches the soul of the reader."

"Beautifully written! I love your vulnerability—thank you for sharing."

"Thank you so much. Thank God there aren't many people who know this kind of pain. But it's also good to know that we aren't alone in our grief... It resonates with my husband and me so much. It's been 44 days since my son took his life. We've never prayed so hard in our lives as we have these last 44 days... Your blog is so insightful. It's not easy sharing this with the world, but my husband (who's been reading it as well) and I are grateful to you for doing so... Thank you again for expressing what those of us behind you on this path are feeling."

"Your journey is so familiar, and your words so vivid and real. Thank you for sharing pieces of Cooper with us."

"You are making it better by sharing your deeply heartfelt story with us. Thank you!"

"Stumbled onto your blog. Your grief is deeply felt in your eloquent blog. My husband and I are eight and a half years out from our son's death. Being able to share your thoughts is powerful. Keep talking and sharing your journey, with your wife, your children, others who you trust with your words. We hear you, we share your brokenness."

"I recently lost my niece, so your blogs are putting words to our grieving as well..."

"Great insights, Kelly. You help others with these posts! One thing I fight with is tremendous guilt. I have since learned that a sudden death typically results in a greater level of guilt and shame—heart-wrenching emotions for sure. Like you, I am slowly but surely remembering the good and trying to be thankful for the ten years we had. Love to you and yours."

"You describe this shadow-casting, coin-collecting gang with such clarity. This particular post hit hard."

"I just want to say I read Kelly's blog, and he has such a gift with words. He puts exactly into words things I've felt for years that I can't explain or get out. Thank you, Kelly. It has been healing for me, the sharing of your blog. Hugs to you and Victoria. I know we are all on this journey of grief, but the important thing to remember is that we are not alone. We have each other."

"I have been really enjoying your blog posts. CJ mentioned to me today that reading them provides comfort, and I agree. It is helpful in my healing process to hear your perspective, thoughts, wonderings, and stories. I mentioned this to CJ today, I think your talent with writing is not something one can learn; it's something you're born with."

"Kelly, your blogs are so powerful to me."

"Kelly, I've enjoyed reading your past blogs—you're such a talented writer. This one speaks to my heart. I pray that the writing process helps with the grief in some way. The way you explained what it's like to have a child missing was surreal, and the sculptures took my breath away. Thanks for sharing. Looking forward to future posts."

disclaimer

I am not a licensed counselor, therapist, or mental health professional. I'm a grieving father, sharing my personal journey through loss and the reflections that have helped me process the grief of losing my son, Cooper. My writing comes from my own experiences, thoughts, and feelings, and it is my way of expressing what I've learned along the way.

Please know that what I share here is not intended as professional counseling, medical advice, or therapy. The content of this book should not be considered a substitute for professional mental health services. I encourage anyone experiencing grief, trauma, or other emotional challenges to seek support from a licensed therapist or counselor, as everyone's healing journey is unique.

Some of the topics discussed in this book may be emotionally intense or triggering for readers who are going through their own grieving process. I urge you to take care of your emotional well-being while reading, and seek support if needed.

Use of this material is at the reader's own discretion and responsibility. If you are in crisis, please call 9-8-8 or 9-1-1.

dedication

For family and friends who have stood with me through the bruises and riptides.

For my mom, who has been making it better and spreading Cooper's kindness her entire life.

For my brother, who walked through hell with me and helped me stand when I could not.

For CJ, Carse, and Grace, who remind me daily of the beauty in resilience and rugged hope. You are free to be surfers, mosaic artists, and carpenters. Full send, go!

For Victoria, who's been Crippin' with me since day one, and is anchored in with me as we navigate the tough spiritual edgework together. I love you.

And for Cooper James, whose memory is woven into every word of this book. You are forever a part of us, and this memoir through grief, resilience, and love, is for you. When it's time for my crane migration, I will see you again, Boy.

contents

Note on Privacy   ix

Introduction   1
I AM   6
By Cooper James (11 years old)

In Memory, Cooper James   7
Cooper James Update   12
Standing Together   15
Spiritual Edgework   19
Rugged Hope   25
Mountains of My Mind   32
40 Days   33
Maine   38
Boys in the Basement   45
Just Breathe and Bruises   51
Crane Migration   53
Crippin   60
Here I Am   66
Red Fox   73
Riptide   79
Made it Better   86
Poundmakers   94
Monk or Millionaire   95
Shadow Casting   107
Aftermath   113
As If   118
Good Grief   121
Cracked Ones   126
Resilience   131
Nearing Six Months   136
Toll For Thee   143
Grief as Negation   151
6 MONTHS   157
By Victoria, Coop's mom

Kindness   159
Grief Fingerprint   163

How Ought a Man to Grieve the Loss of His
Child?   170

Hedgehogs   175

Freezing   177

Alters   181

Wrecked   183

EI   188

Thinking of You, Cooper Spotify Playlist   192

Free Write   193

SPREAD COOPER KINDNESS   201
By Nanny Kathy, Coop's grandmother

I LOVE YOU   206
By Jason, Coop's uncle

Surfers, Mosaic Artists, and Carpenters   210

Theological Three Sisters   217

JUST TO BE WITH YOU   227
By Victoria, Coop's mom

Honoring Cooper   234

Acknowledgments   239

Endnotes   242

Appendix A   246

Appendix B   253

Appendix C   258

About the Author   263

note on privacy

To respect the privacy of individuals and places, some names, locations, and identifying details have been changed in this book. While the events and experiences shared here are true to my journey, certain elements have been modified to protect the privacy of those involved.

However, my son Cooper James' real name and identity have been kept unchanged. This decision is intentional and meant to honor his memory and the deep impact he continues to have on so many lives.

introduction

W e live in a small Midwestern college town. On October 7th, 2023, our university football team played an out of conference rival. My wife and I attended a pre-game tailgate party near the football stadium with several friends. We were parked on a small hill overlooking the stadium.

It was a beautiful fall day, the kind where your body feels the seasons shifting, a certain sparkle on the skin. The temperature hovered in the low 70s, the sky was clear, the winds calm, and the surrounding trees blazed with orange, yellow, and red, as if preparing to welcome the winter. It was the perfect day for football.

Around 2 PM, our son, Cooper, 23, arrived at the tailgate party with two friends. I didn't speak with him directly, giving him space to be with his buddies. I watched him eat two hamburgers, drink a beer, and chat with one of the adults, answering questions about his relatively new job at the university. He seemed relaxed, I saw him smile. What more could a father want than to see his son enjoying himself on such a day?

At 3 PM, my wife and I left the tailgate and headed home, as we didn't have tickets to the game. We've never been big college football fans. Cooper had tickets, though, and as he left with his friends to enter the stadium, he turned to wave goodbye to his mom.

What we didn't know was that it would be the last time we saw him.

While most people were reading about the massacre in Israel on the morning of October 8th, we were receiving news that would shatter our world into a trillion pieces.

Two law enforcement officers and a chaplain arrived at our front door with the news no parent ever wants to hear.

Our youngest son, Cooper James, 23 years old, had taken his own life near a local conservation area.

Scorched earth.

We couldn't breathe, we couldn't stand. The pain and confusion felt like a micro-atomic bomb had been dropped on our home.

In the weeks that followed, amid the rubble of our lives, I instinctively turned to writing. I can't fully explain why it was my first impulse, but something deep inside drove me to put my pain into words, to try to capture the bone-crushing grief of child loss. Writing became my way of sifting through the chaos, my attempt to hold up the pieces of my shattered heart and shake my fists at the Universe.

I was never a great student in high school. Not because I lacked aptitude, but because I lacked the right academic attitude. I felt trapped in those classrooms, yearning to be anywhere else— skiing, laughing, partying. Yet, unbeknownst to most people, I had a hidden talent for writing, something only my high school English teacher recognized.

On the last day of high school, she called me into her office and told me plainly, "Kelly, you're wasting your talent. You're an excellent writer."

For more than 30 years, that comment lived in the back of my mind. Someday, I thought, I'll write. Someday, I'll use my voice to tell my story.

When Cooper died, that "someday" became "now." My soul clicked on, and I knew it was time to write.

Initially, this book began as a letter to family and friends, sharing the news of Cooper's death. I wrote a piece titled *In Memory, Cooper James*, saved it as a PDF, and emailed it to those close to us. A week later, I wrote another update, *Cooper James Update*, and shared it in the same way.

The feedback was surprising—people told me I had something important to say, and I was encouraged to share more publicly.

That's when the idea of a blog[1] came about. Writing became a way not only to express my grief but to try to prevent this kind of tragedy from happening to others. I also wondered if, as a retired firefighter, I could use my voice to bring other men into the conversation about grief and healing, to show that it's okay for men to hurt, to cry, and to grieve openly.

This book is the evolution of those early letters and blog posts. It's a collection of raw, unfiltered writing that traces my journey through the first year of child loss—October 2023 to October 2024. There are no easy answers here, no neat resolutions. Just questions, pain, and endurance.

If you've lost a child, I don't need to explain anything to you— you already know. If you've lost a deep love—a sibling, a grand-child, a parent, a partner, a dear friend—you are in the arena with me. You have a sense of what it means to navigate this kind of loss.

For those who haven't experienced deep loss, my hope is that these pages offer a window into what it feels like to experience profound grief. It's not pretty, but it's real.

This book won't provide solutions. I don't understand why Cooper made the choice he did, and I probably never will. What this book does offer is a witness to what it's like to endure the unendurable.

Each chapter is a step in this long journey toward healing. It's resilience and rugged hope in action. It's the process of learning to live with a broken heart.

I hope that for those who read this book, you find in these pages a sense of companionship, a recognition of the shared human experience of grief and loss. We go in together; we come out together. If you go, we go.

If you're one of those, like us, who has lost a child, sibling, or grandchild, you are not alone in your grief and sorrow, your brokenness, your despair, and your evolving transformation into the new you. We get it.

We understand that a demarcation line has been drawn. There's the old you before your loss, and the new you after.

For those who knew Cooper, I hope this book honors his life. It's one of the ways I hope to remember the beautiful, brilliant, kind-hearted young man he was. For those who didn't know Cooper, I hope you come to see, through these words, the light that he was in our lives and the love that we have for him.

I don't know why, but our family has been called to endure the unendurable. This book captures what endurance looks like.

Thank you for joining us on this journey through the first year of child loss—it's not an easy one. We love you, Son.

i am

November 28, 2011

By Cooper James (11 years old)

I am awesome and miniature.
I wonder if global warming is true.
I hear the air conditioner humming.
I see the world.
I want Christmas to come quicker.
I am awesome and miniature.

I pretend to play for FC Barcelona.
I feel lonely when I'm alone.
I touch the soccer ball.
I worry about the homeless.
I cry when I am sad.
I am awesome and miniature.

I understand why I go to school.
I say "ow!" when I get hurt.
I dream about soccer.
I try to practice soccer.
I hope to become smarter.
I am awesome and miniature.

in memory, cooper james
October 14, 2023

Dear Family and Friends,

We write this letter in deep, aching soul pain. Our youngest son, Cooper James, 23, took his own life in the early morning of Sunday, October 8th, near a local conservation area.

Cooper grew up in Southern Arizona, playing club and high school soccer. He graduated from "The Ridge" and attended the University of Arizona, majoring in Aerospace Engineering, graduating in May 2022.

Cooper James

Shortly after graduation, Cooper was hired by a university in the Midwest, working in the School of Engineering.

Cooper lived with us over the past year, learning his new job and saving money.

For those who knew Cooper well, you know he was a sweet,

gentle soul. Everyone, without exception, loved him. He was pleasant and easy to be around.

Cooper was an animal lover, especially fond of our family dogs—Snoopy, Bear Bear, and Willow. Snoopy, 13, was Cooper's dog. Cooper also had a quirky fondness for hedgehogs.

Cooper's closest friend growing up was Ethan. If we didn't know better, we would say Ethan's family had a third son for many years.

Cooper wore a Hebrew bracelet throughout his college days that roughly translates to, "a man is a man is a man." Meaning, we're all humans in the end.

Living at home with us over the past year, Cooper was able to spend quality time with his grandfather, Poppy Jack, before his passing from Parkinson's disease in May 2023. Poppy Jack was proud that Cooper worked at his alma mater.

Cooper was actively flying Cessna airplanes and was close to securing his private pilot's license. He recently made a cross country flight.

Cooper enjoyed golfing on weekends, spending time at the lake and local conservation area hiking, and driving around in his new Honda Civic, checking out the sights. Cooper enjoyed living in a small college town and spending time on the college boulevard eating, drinking, and hanging out.

Over the last year, Cooper began lifting weights religiously, becoming big and strong. He was also teaching himself guitar, improving steadily, and taking French lessons one night per week. As Cooper lived with us, we noticed how much structure and routine mattered to him.

We don't know why Cooper took his life. We can look back and see a few red flags, but nothing glaring. We have many unanswered questions and tremendous guilt. While we don't know for sure, we are beginning to shape some contours that feel like this:

Cooper didn't use drugs and rarely drank. He was a gentle, sensitive soul living in a harsh world. He was hard on himself—a perfectionist. College was especially hard on Cooper. While brilliant (his IQ was high), he was socially introverted. This made it difficult for him to make new friends and form intimate relationships—from his perspective. This social introversion led to feelings of loneliness and isolation. The two years of COVID-19 messaging—"socially distance and isolate"—during Cooper's last two years of college compounded these feelings. Layered on top of this is likely undiagnosed depression and generalized anxiety, combined with social anxiety. It's likely growing up as a digital native, that technology and social media contributed to Cooper's anxiety and depression. This created a heavy load. Cooper was in a lot of pain, enduring more than any of us realized.

We don't know if the above initial sketch is "correct" or not. We'll never know for sure, but it's all we have right now—it's the best we can come up with. As parents drowning in grief, we naturally seek answers.

We long and ache to know what happened, but more than anything, we want a do-over, a chance to get it right. The finality of this event is crushing, and the pain immense. It doesn't seem like it was supposed to happen; we feel like the Universe got it wrong. We want our son back.

As we look back at pictures of Cooper over the years, it's clear to us that Cooper did have a good life, with many good times and memories made with family and friends. We see his smile, the twinkle in his eye, a gentle smirk, and genuine happiness.

We held a short memorial service for Cooper at our house on October 12th, with close family present. It was stunningly beautiful and perfect, bringing a sense of peace to our home. We later visited Cooper at the funeral home and spent time with his body—honoring him, touching him, and saying goodbye. It was the kind of experience that sucks the air from your lungs and drops you to your knees but was so necessary in our healing process. Cooper's brothers, CJ and Carse, his sister Grace, sister-in-law Em, and grandparents Lois, Kathy, and James were with us. We left Snoopy's collar and a rosary in his hands and prayed deeply for him and over him.

Cooper and his beloved dog, Snoopy

So where do we go from here?

We are not sure whether to cremate or bury Cooper. Oddly, it's a tough decision because we never gave it much thought. If buried, Cooper will be laid to rest where his grandfather Jack and great-grandparents are buried. In that case, we'll purchase plots next to his and be buried with him in the future.

Many have asked how they can help or where they can donate. Given Cooper's love and fondness for animals, especially dogs, we ask family and friends to donate in memory of Cooper to your local animal shelter/humane society.

We clearly have a long, painful road of grief and recovery ahead. Our family will never be the same. How could it?

The best thing you can do for us right now is to hold Cooper's loving memory with you always. Keep his gentle light alive in your heart. Say his name, remember him, smile for him. Pray for him, and pray for us.

We need to end the stigma surrounding mental health and wellness. There is no shame in seeking counseling and establishing baseline medical care (labs) with your family doctor. Sadly, self-harm is endemic in our society, and we are not doing enough to help young men.

Finally, in case you didn't know, the U.S. has a relatively new 9-8-8 suicide and crisis hotline for mental health emergencies. Learn the number, know it, and share it.

Thank you for your prayers.

Kelly & Victoria

~

cooper james update

October 23, 2023

Dear family and friends,

Together, as a family, we made the decision to bury Cooper. He was laid to rest next to his grandfather, Poppy Jack, and his great-grandparents, on October 20th.

Victoria and I purchased two plots next to Cooper's, and someday, we will be buried next to our son. When we next visit the cemetery, I will get the latitude and longitude coordinates and send them. If any of Cooper's friends or family decide to take a road trip, let us know, and you can stay with us. The cemetery is 1.5 hours from our home.

The funeral* was a small graveside service with immediate family present. I delivered the service. I aimed for a Christian, experiential, affective service. An invocation for God to be with us was made. Family members were anointed with oil for healing. We read Psalm 23 together: *"Yea, though I walk through the valley of the shadow of death, I will fear no evil; for You are with me; Your rod and Your staff, they comfort me."* We borrowed from the Quaker

---

* Appendix A: Outline of Cooper's Funeral

tradition and spent time in silence. Cooper was eulogized. The gravesite was blessed with holy water. We circled the casket, holding hands, and prayed the Lord's Prayer together. Each of us placed a handful of dirt on top of the casket, symbolizing ashes to ashes, dust to dust. The song "Memorial" by Ike Ndolo was played.

We can't say why exactly we chose burial over cremation. As we joked, 'the little man inside us' (Seinfeld) was simply telling us it was more appropriate for our family to bury Cooper. So we followed that still, small voice.

Cooper

We didn't do embalming, no vault, and we opted for a biodegradable casket. We imagine years from now, Cooper will quite literally become the grass, the trees, the insects, and the birds of the air. The full circle of life, playing out on a little hill, on a prairie, in the Midwest—with the blades of grass waving their prayers and the bugs reflecting the sunlight as it slices through the trees.

Before Cooper was buried, we took Snoopy, his dog, to see him. Snoopy sniffed a lot, placed his paw on Cooper's arm, but didn't seem distraught. We just wanted Snoopy to know that Cooper wasn't coming home. We had one last chance to anoint Cooper's body with olive oil, frankincense, rosemary, and cinnamon.

We are learning that trying times bring out the weird. We talk to Cooper as if he's still with us, sit in his living room, touch his guitar, books, and wallet. We smell the room like we're drawing him in. We light candles every morning, crack the back door so his soul can enter, and so on. We imagine this is normal?

The first week was a traumatic madhouse. Our foundation gave way. Things have calmed down; we're doing better. Today is the second day all family has been gone—now it's me, Victoria, Grace, and Grandma Lois. It's obvious Cooper is missing; the void is palpable. We stand at the window with long, blank stares, barely noticing the trees changing colors and the leaves falling.

Did the change of seasons factor into this?

I remember hiking in the mountains once. I sat in a beautiful clearing and wanted my life to look like that—beautiful. Shortly up the hill, I came across a mangled gulley where water and lightning had left a mess. I stood there for a long time before I could see it, but I finally did. Despite the devastation, there was life—moss, bugs, birds, new growth.

Already, we've seen beauty in this tragedy. Our family, friends, and coworkers (especially from my wife's local school community) have shown us great love and care. Your condolences, wonderful food, flowers, cards, art, candles, and the general compassion you've shown us have held us up when it's been difficult to stand or function on our own. For this, we are grateful.

With gratitude,

Kelly & Victoria, CJ & Em, Carse, Grace

- and Cooper

~

standing together

The flowers have mostly run their course. A few bouquets, late in coming, are still alive with color but are beginning to wilt. The food is eaten, and various snacks litter the kitchen counter—even in grief, there are limits to how many snacks one can eat in good conscience.

The beautiful, heartfelt cards have slowed in arriving. Text messages are scant, and the emails are gone too. My phone rings less. I frequently talk with my wife, daughter, and mom—a little less so with my brother—and I stay in touch with our sons living out of state. They are not big talkers.

I knew this day would come, but the silence—the "bounce," as my neighbor describes it—arrived more quickly than I anticipated. Most family and friends want to get on with their lives, regain their own balance, and move forward. This is completely understandable; I would too.

Understand, we (my wife and I) can't move forward that fast. To be fair, I am okay with this period of relative silence. I need the time and space to process, reflect, and grieve. It's important to me, in honor of my son, that I make as much sense of this as I can. I am spending a lot of time going through Cooper's digital history, looking for clues, trying to make sense of things. In fact, there are some things coming up that, while hard, are filling in the gaps.

My wife is home; she has been off work from teaching her "littles," as have I, and we spend a lot of time together talking and reflecting. We tend to end up talking in circles sometimes, but I think this is okay. We are processing together. While I am weepy in the morning, my wife is weepy in the evening. We are working through our grief in different ways and at different speeds. I need to make sense of this, while my wife spends time looking at pictures and feeling. I create timelines and read through texts and emails; my wife sends pictures for printing at Walgreens.

I am still shocked by how suddenly Cooper vanished. He was here one moment and gone the next. I had a hamburger and a beer with him Saturday at a tailgate party, and then Sunday morning, he was gone. As I previously wrote, the finality of losing him is crushing. Man, it hurts. It hurts me too because I know, I believe, with quality therapy and good medical care there more than likely would have been a different outcome.

Friends ask, "How are you doing?" In truth, I think I am doing okay. I am being sincere. As I respond to this question when it's asked, I wonder: what's the barometer for losing a child, the gauge, to know how you are really doing? What is my basis of comparison? While I think I am doing "okay," I have no past life experience to draw from, comparable with this event. None of my life experiences can begin to compare with this enormous blow.

Friends, I will explore counseling or grief therapy; I am not against it. My wife has already scheduled a meeting with a counselor. She's on it, and I applaud her. I am still "feeling"—not thinking—about how I want to process this loss in the manner best for me.

Some days, I just feel like getting in the car and driving for a long, long time. A road trip. Road trips allow for that quiet processing time, just thinking it through.

Sure, I have had hard times in my life. I wonder if hard time x 1, plus hard time x 2, plus hard time x 3 creates an ability to deal with hard times no matter the context? I mean to say, I have had some steeling in my life, and I think this has helped me.

I am walking 30 minutes per day, eating decent food in reasonable amounts, drinking water, sleeping reasonably well, reading, praying, and otherwise caring for myself and my family. My wife is doing the same. Oddly, I do find that I am drinking coffee throughout the entire day—this is new for me. It seems I have to have something in my hand.

I have a morning routine. I get up, take the dogs out, pick up the house a bit, and start the coffee. I am still cracking the window and turning the lights on in Cooper's room, you know, so his soul can visit. I light a candle and say my prayers for Cooper and for all of our family and friends, for healing in this grief.

Our long, wooden dining room table has become an altar. Pictures of Cooper, crosses, ceramic cardinals, watercolor paintings, angels, candles, the Bible, and flowers cover the table. This is where I say my morning prayers, after lighting the candle for the day.

Alter on dining room table

I am functioning, but I do notice I have a diminished capacity for sustained cognitive activity and remembering. I can't work through mental complexity as I normally would. My usually poor listening skills are at an all-time low. What?

My emotions come in waves, and they are difficult to name. I am not sure how to describe these emotions showing up in my body. I am dealing with feelings I have never had before.

On some days, I feel good. I have hope for a brighter future in the midst of this suffering. I know there is a positive future ahead of me. I say a new mantra out loud to myself, "The best days of my life are ahead of me." I know I am sort of lying to myself in saying this, but my brain is pretty naive. It believes the things I tell it, funnily, even when it knows it is being deceived.

In some moments, on given days, I do realize with absolute clarity what a huge, life-shattering event this really is, and I can't even hide it from myself. The magnitude of losing my son hits me hard, and I weep in my grief. I loved him, I miss him, and I am heartbroken that he was in so much pain and I did not know the depth of it. He was such a good soul with such a bright future ahead of him.

I know this sudden, tragic event has impacted many, many people—friends and family. We, as parents, are not the only ones grieving. All of us are. We all hurt, and I know this.

Here we are then, standing together. And I think, if I didn't know any better, that for today, standing together is a noble act.

spiritual edgework
November 10, 2023

During my fire department career, I was not on a special operations team. These are the teams conducting specialized rescues, like swift water rescue, confined space rescue, and high-angle rescue. I did receive "operations" level training in these disciplines and later became a rope rescue technician.

After my fire department career in Arizona, we moved to Montana. I was a faculty member in the Fire Science program at Montana State University Billings. My wife was a 1st grade teacher in the public schools. Because tuition was low-cost for faculty, I decided to take a few courses I thought would be "fun." They were fun; I loved them. I took courses in Search & Rescue, Wilderness First Responder, and Rock Climbing I. In Montana, these are next-level courses—they are legit.

With my educational background and experience in fire department leadership, I was also teaching a few leadership courses in the Outdoor Adventure Leadership program.

As I learned more about search and rescue in the backcountry, I applied and interviewed to become a Volunteer Search & Rescue Technician with a Fire/Rescue Department near the Beartooth

Mountains. I was accepted and began training. I did not finish the volunteer training program before moving to the Midwest, but I was able to complete some excellent search and rescue training, including avalanche rescue training.

I share the above to highlight a sociological theory called "edgework," and how I have been thinking about this concept in the last few days as I continue to process my grief, sadness, and sorrow following Cooper's death. I am not steeped in the theory of edgework; I only know it as a concept. As my Israeli friend, Eitan, says, "Let's not let details ruin a good story, shall we?"

Edgework was originally applied to thrill-seekers pushing their physical limits right up to the edge of life and death. When you watch a Warren Miller ski film or big wave surfers, this is edgework in the physical realm. This was the original intent of the language. The rush of thrill-seekers is held right on the edge of life and death.

Jen Lois, a search and rescue technician in Colorado and researcher, began to apply this term to the emotional dynamics that search and rescue technicians experience in their work.[1] She moved the meaning away from physicality and toward the mental and emotional realm. She wondered how rescuers bring their emotions and minds to the upper limits of functioning under extreme stress in backcountry rescue[2].

Good rescuers need to be in mental and emotional control. They need to know their limits and recognize when they are nearing them. A rescuer beyond their upper limits serves nobody well; they become a liability and may even need rescuing, creating a greater problem—an unfortunate cascade.

Good rescuers are not thrill-seekers. This is not unlike firefighting. I never considered myself a thrill-seeker during my fire department career; quite the opposite, actually. I—we—took a very calculated approach to saving lives. There were a few times when my work took me to the edge—physically, mentally, and emotionally. In fact, upon my retirement after 25 years of service, I experienced being mentally and emotionally over the edge, and it took me a good eight months to right myself. Stress injury is for real.

In the immediate aftermath of Cooper's death, one of my initial responses was to want to chase after him into the spirit realms. No, I did not want to end my life. I have always enjoyed living, and I still do today. It was my hardwiring as a firefighter coming out—I wanted to attempt a rescue, spiritually. If there was a thin space I could jump into and do battle with the spirits to bring Cooper back, I was willing. I was willing to fight a spiritual fire, if only I could.

Further, I did not want my son going it alone. I was trafficking in the maxim from *Backdraft*, the firefighting movie: "If you go, we go." It pained me—it still pains me—that Cooper left this world alone. I know, I know. People tell me he was not alone, the Heavenlies were with him. I pray it so, but nevertheless, there was not another person in the flesh and blood with him. This greatly bothers me.

Of course, we live in reality, and there is no unwinding the clock. What is done is done. While I cannot unwind the clock, I have gone back in my spiritual imagination and prayed for Cooper in that moment, imagining I was with him. Call it holy mysticism. Yes, I know he's still going to do his thing, and I can't stop him, but in this spiritual imagining, he's not alone; I am holding his hand. I don't try to stop him, I am simply with him. This idea, of praying back in time to be with Cooper in that moment, came through a counselor with Red Bird Ministries.[3] I recently had a "comfort call" with her, and she presented this idea as we were talking. It resonated with me.

For today, and the last few weeks, I feel like what I have been doing is spiritual edgework. I keep coming back to a memory I have of setting up an anchoring system for rock climbing and rappelling. I am standing right on the edge of rock, anchored in, with Cooper. He's getting ready to rappel. We are safe, but not entirely without risk. I am not alone. We are standing together on the edge. It's a great day. We are together—no cell phones. Just a father, his son, and their hands, in nature, sun on the skin.

Cooper and Dad rappelling

I know, because I am living it, any person who has lost someone special to them due to unexpected loss, especially suicide, is doing edgework every day in the immediate aftermath of their loss. It's precarious spiritual space to be in.

We are standing on a spiritual edge, hopefully anchored in, hopefully not alone, peeking over into the abyss wondering what's on the other side of this thin space, where did our loved one go, and why?

We might say, "God, Universe, Creator, I am not angry, but please, do tell." We might add, "I may, in the future, be angry, and You will surely know, but for today, I am vexed."

I made a comment in my last post about standing together as a noble act. I believe this.

I think it's interesting that standing, feet shoulder-width apart, with a firm feeling of being grounded, together with others who I know care, on the edge of a cliff, is the image I have during this phase of grief.

I know I am doing spiritual edgework, poking around in spiritual areas. Some of these areas feel comfortable; others feel tenuous. As I noted, part of being a good "rescuer" is knowing your limits and stepping back from the edge. I have done this on a few occasions.

I am not thrill-seeking. I am meaning-making—trying.

The truth is, I know I am never really going to know for sure why Cooper took his own life. As I have read through Cooper's accessible data (that I have been able to gain access to), I have gained a fuller, though not a complete, picture. What I have is a charcoal sketch, rough in the outline. I am feeling some level of contentment with this. One, I love charcoal sketches. But two, I feel I have done the due diligence I will be able to do with this chapter of the Unfolding.

What I most miss in this exploration of the spiritual edge, besides being with my son, is a faith-wisdom community—more anchors. Given the vicissitudes of life—COVID-19, moving to a new town—we have not yet established a faith-wisdom community to grow and worship with, to explore with. I am greatly sensing this gap in our life right now. This is an area I (we) need to shore up—mental note to self; and, no pun intended for the rescue audience.

How am I doing? I think okay. I have been doing spiritual edge-work, I have not been alone, I am anchored in, and I have a healthy respect for my spiritual limits, including mental and emotional limits. My feet are shoulder-width apart, I am grounded, but I have been on the edge. I am comfortable here, peering over, wondering *"where's Cooper?"*

I pray you are doing well. Safe edge-working to you. Let me know if you need an anchor. I am here for you too.

rugged hope
November 13, 2023

I can't help but to question my parenting following Cooper's death.

What parent wouldn't have questions, guilt, and a host of "what if we had done this, what if we had done that, what if we had zigged there instead of zagging?"

I understand that could have, would have, should have is normal in grief.

I am a student of resilience science. I have also been a teacher of resilience at the university. In my past studies, there's a particular phrase I have come across that is ringing quite loudly in my mind: "good enough" parenting or caregiving (Dr. Michael Ungar).[1]

Resilience is rarely about an individual person and their personal grit. Grit matters little. Thirty years of international, cross-cultural research demonstrates convincingly that resilience is about the resources and support we have access to in our times of adversity and trauma—times like this.

For example, I am not "doing okay" right now because I have gritty personal qualities. I am doing okay, marginally, because I live in a comfortable house, in a safe community, and we have been supported by family, friends, coworkers, and a faith-wisdom leader. We are doing okay because we have access to counselors and have had time off work to process and begin to heal. We have health insurance. We have a car to drive to appointments. We have money to pay co-pays. We have coffee and craft beer. We have snacks and lots of chocolate.

Dad and Cooper

For resilient outcomes, one "resource" we all need, which makes it easier to deal with tough times in life, is "good enough" parenting. To be clear, people do have resilient outcomes even if they didn't (or don't) have good enough parenting, but this likely means they have other resources that compensate.

As I think about Cooper and his upbringing, nurture and nature, how we raised him, and where we raised him, I can say, almost unequivocally, that our parenting of Cooper was "good enough." You notice my lack of complete confidence. I notice it too.

Writing "almost unequivocally" makes me chuckle to myself, and I suppose in this moment, I am glad to be laughing.

Here's what I am expressing: I have guilt that my child took his own life. As I puzzle over why he did it, I can't help but question my parenting. Where was I at play in his death? Where am I responsible and culpable? The old Episcopalian prayer comes to mind: "What have I done, and what have I left undone?"

As I think about resilience, resources, and Cooper, I do know with reasonable certainty that our parenting was "good enough." I have a high level of confidence in this. Great parenting? Probably not. As all parents know, they don't hand you a child-raising manual when you leave the hospital. You simply do the best you can at the time. Sadly, we tend to bring our own childhood dysfunction to the family dynamic, which makes great parenting difficult. And oh, by the way, who is the judge of great parenting? I like models. Show me a model of great parenting.

Now that I am thinking more clearly and have more space in my brain, I am beginning to read books on grief and healing following child loss. I didn't get my first book purchase right for our particular situation, because it doesn't deal with child loss per se, but I did enjoy reading *The Deepest Place: Suffering and the Formation of Hope*[2] by Curt Thompson, MD.

I am very quickly learning, in the thick of the grief of child loss, that "resilience," as I know it and teach it, is not enough. I am experiencing that there is another domain beyond resilience—meta-resilience—and it is hope. I now believe the formation of rugged hope is more important than resilience. Rugged hope, I think, is only born in the crucible of tremendous suffering.

When the micro-atomic bomb dropped on our house Sunday, October 8th, in the weeks following, it felt to me like the most important thing was to somehow sense, know, see, and feel there will be a better future. Otherwise, this is a f**king joke.

There will be better days, I know. My two boys, my daughter, and their bright futures are some things I am looking forward to. I am hopeful in figuring out our new future together with my wife following this devastation. We are not making any major changes for at least a year, but maybe we will go travel the world, who knows. I really want to visit Finland. Maybe we launch. Not saying we are going to do this; I am painting future possibilities to give us a glimpse of hope.

In his book, Dr. Thompson brings up secure attachment theory as necessary for forming hope, and he describes secure attachment through the 4 S's: being Seen, Soothed, Safe, and Secure.

I think back to Cooper, especially his formative years, the last four years, the last year, even the last weeks of his life, and I ask myself: Was Cooper seen, soothed, safe, and secure in his relationship with his mother, father, brothers, sister, close family, and friends? Again, I believe with a high level of confidence, the answer is yes. Cooper was definitively seen, he was soothed, he was safe, and he was secure with his family and close friends.

Sadly, I don't know if Cooper was seen, soothed, safe, and secure with others outside of the home. I would like to hope so.

Just know, every person we come into contact with on a given day could be in a very isolated and lonely place, very hurt, and our smile, our seeing them, may prevent further micro-atomic bombs being dropped on families.

On the Sunday morning Cooper took his life, my brother was in Florida on vacation with friends. When he learned about Cooper, he flew into town to be with us. He arrived late Sunday night. I honestly don't know what I would have done without my brother here in those early days. He slept on the floor next to me all night for four nights, and we woke up throughout the night crying, talking, and sometimes standing up and hugging it out. My brother told his friends, "I need to leave and go walk through hell with my brother." And he did. He stood in the center of the fire with me and did not shirk back. He left my house in tatters—it really was true hell.

One of the mornings, as we had coffee, my brother said, "Here are two things you need to know: 1) you loved your son and he loved you, and 2) you did the absolute best you could." He was not asking me a question. He was making a statement; he was commanding me to hear him. As you can read, I did.

Kelly and Jason, brothers

I have libertarian ethos tendencies. I do.

My great-grandfather was a miner and worked the copper mines in Butte, Montana. My grandfather was born in Butte. Growing up, my dad always said, "Live and let live."

It was not until we lived in Montana for a few years that I was able to pick up on the underlying philosophy my dad was always preaching. Not unsurprisingly, I too share this philosophy. Live and let live.

Cooper was his own man, a created being in the image of God, *imago dei*, with his own eternal soul. He was the Captain of his ship, the master of his fate. As his father, I frequently counseled him, but I never forced him to do anything.

I counseled Cooper to "go pro" several times, to get professional counseling, and to see a doctor about getting baseline labs drawn. I gave Cooper a list of possible counselors and doctors to choose from, the ones covered by insurance, highly recommended he go see them, and then stood back. This goes back to the college days when he was having a tough go of it.

For some reason, it seems important for a lot of people around me to tell me that Cooper's death is not my fault and that I shouldn't feel guilty. I'm not a counselor nor trained in this profession, so they must have some reason for saying this to me.

What I have done here is share why I should not have guilt over Cooper taking his life. But again, if you have been reading my blog, I know my own tomfoolery, the tricks I am telling myself.

Friends, it's okay; I accept, in the main, my own arguments here.

- Cooper surely had good enough parenting. I sincerely believe this.
- Cooper was seen, soothed, safe, and secure with his parents, siblings, and close family and friends.
- I loved my son, he loved me, and I did the absolute best I could in parenting him. My wife, the same. Brothers, the same. Sister, the same. Close family and friends, the same.
- I always treated Cooper as a unique, creative, intelligent, caring individual created in the image of God and capable of making his own choices. I nurtured his self-agency. I trusted his free will and did not impose myself upon him in a strict manner. I acted as mentor and confidant, especially as he grew older.

I believe all of the above, and it is true. But please, can you fault me (us) for having some level of guilt and remorse over this? This seems natural to me, to have these questions and guilt.

No matter. In my suffering, I do have hope for a brighter future. "The best days of my life are ahead of me."

I pray the same for you. I am glad you exist, and I am excited for your future.

mountains of my mind
November 14, 2023

My wife, the good mom and woman, is back to school teaching the littles. All things considered, she's doing well. She's crushed in the deep places, I know, and she will never be the same, but I'm really amazed at how well she's navigating this tragic life event. She had her first counseling session yesterday and really liked her therapist. It went well.

I went for a walk today, part of my daily therapy, and decided against listening to audiobooks. Everybody's preaching, and none of it is landing well with me. There's too much noise, too many voices. I have to think about who I want to listen to. Narrow focus for me.

Instead, I decided to listen to Chris Stapleton's new album, *Higher.*[1] It's an excellent album. Below are two songs that leveled me as I listened to the lyrics in relation to Cooper. Real tears.

> - *Mountains of My Mind,* Chris Stapleton
> - *Weight of Your World,* Chris Stapleton

~

40 days

November 16, 2023

Forty days is a spiritually significant number. I don't know why.

- It rained for 40 days and 40 nights – Old Testament
- Moses was on Mount Sinai for 40 days and 40 nights – Old Testament
- Elijah fasted for 40 days and 40 nights – Old Testament
- Jesus fasted and was tempted in the desert for 40 days and 40 nights – New Testament

I could go on. The Bible, Scripture, is filled with 40-day symbolism.

Across all religions, the number 40 is spiritually significant. For example, Buddha sat under the Bodhi tree for 40 days and 40 nights before experiencing Nirvana (some say 49 days; but let's not let details ruin a good story…).

Tomorrow, November 17th, marks 40 days since Cooper's death. It is customary in our religious tradition to offer special prayers for the dead on the 40th day of their death.

As I have shared, over the last 39 days, I have cracked the window in the house, left the light on, lit candles, and I have been offering prayers throughout the day for Cooper. I say his name, I talk about him, I remember the good times.

There is a group of women in Tubac, Arizona, family friends, whom my mom calls the "prayer warriors." They have been praying for Cooper relentlessly.

Prayers for Cooper make a difference. Following the thread of my breath down to the bottom place, I believe this.

God is the breath in the breath.

CJ, Grace, Cooper, Victoria, Carse

In my prayers, I frequently ask the already departed—Cooper's grandparents, family, and friends—to guide him and protect him, to show him the way home.

I reach out in prayer to my departed friends, a firefighter and a retired Marine, men who I know are battle-tested, and I ask them for their help in protecting and watching over my son in the Heavenly places. Because I know these men, and their hard-wiring, I know that if they can, they will.

My prayer for Cooper, his soul, is rather simple; spiritual minimalism.

I pray for Cooper's peace. It's clear Cooper was not at peace. I want him to know peace down to the pinpoint atom center of his soul, and then infused throughout. Perfect bliss.

I pray for his happiness. A big, fat smile that never leaves. The face of his soul hurts because he can't stop smiling.

I pray he knows and is surrounded by infinite love. The kind of love that makes you cry because it's so overwhelming in its goodness.

I pray he is protected from the Harry Potter Dementors, and whatever the equivalent is *del otro lado*.

You must understand, I believe every person has an eternal soul that will never, ever die. When the soul separates from the physical body at death, it necessarily goes somewhere.

It's why, when I was recently asked how many children I have, I answered four. I do have four children, one just happens to live in the spiritual realm these days. I will see Cooper again.

I believe Cooper, his soul, is with the Trinitarian God—that is, the Father, Son (Jesus), and Holy Spirit. I cannot prove this to you. Now you understand why it's called "faith." I am hoping and seeing, sensing, what is unseen.

But my (our) faith is not unreasoned and uninformed. I arrive at my faith partly through intellect, yes, but mainly through my heart, spirit, and will. I understand and accept my intellect has an upper limit where it no longer comprehends the spiritual dimensions.

In Cooper's death, I am sensing with my heart. My daily prayer work arises from my spirit. This is not physical, intellectual, or emotional labor; this is spiritual labor.

I've never worked so hard.

Friends, as we approach day 40, I would like to ask for your help. Many of you have stated, "Please, let us know what you need, if you need anything at all..."

I accept your grace, and I ask for your prayers for Cooper's soul today and tomorrow as we approach a spiritually significant cairn.

I am asking you to pray my simple prayer for Cooper, or please, pray your own prayers. Light a candle for Cooper, say his name, smile, remember him, tell good stories—he has some good ones.

I want to let the Universe know Cooper matters. I want to shake the foundations a bit.

Short Cooper Story

We educated all of our children in the primary grades at a local Montessori school. My wife and I have a great appreciation and fondness for all things Montessori.

One day, Cooper went to Montessori—this was in preschool or kindergarten—and the teacher noticed he was picking at his crotch all morning. He could not get comfortable.

The teacher took Cooper to the restroom to see what was going on. What was going on is that Cooper had heisted his brother's Silly Putty and packed it in his underwear.

You can imagine a big wad of flattened Silly Putty sitting in Cooper's underwear up against his stuff, and understand why he was picking at himself all morning.

Coop

maine
November 19, 2023

W ell, we passed the 40-day mark. Beyond the spiritual significance of 40 days, this marker provided an opportunity to assess how we are doing in our healing process.

How are we doing?

This continues to be an interesting question to me because I don't have a mental scaffolding to anchor it to. I don't have a basis of comparison in my mind or heart. That said, I'm going to stick to the narrative I've been sharing: "I think we are doing okay." True story.

We're functioning reasonably well. We have our moments, for sure. We are eating, drinking, bathing, sleeping, talking to others, and getting out of the house more frequently. Are we back to our normal routines? Not really. In fairness, I don't imagine our routines will ever be the same. We are developing new routines.

One of the most important concepts I learned early on in this tragedy is that everyone grieves differently and at different paces. My good neighbors shared this with me. It sounds simple, and it is, but understanding this concept helps take the edge off what grieving is "supposed" to look like. There is no pressure to meet an arbitrary expectation of how we are supposed to be doing at any given point in time.

There's no right way to grieve, and it takes the time it takes.

Cooper

I met with a licensed counselor last week. It was an unofficial, official visit. Let me explain. This counselor is a former coworker, and he met with me as a professional courtesy and because he's a nice man. I am not directly under his care long-term. I will, however, continue to check in and meet with him periodically over the next couple of months to see how things are going. If I need long-term care, he will help point me in the right direction. I think, for now, this is all I need. Or maybe this is all I want right now. This is more in line with the peer support model used in the fire service, a model I have familiarity and comfort with.

He did say he was happy with the "array" of things I was doing. The array of things I am doing includes writing (such as this blog), meaning-making (creating a timeline), a morning routine honoring Cooper (candles, prayers), frequently talking to my wife and mom about this event, and staying connected to my children and helping them process their emotions.

Meanwhile, my wife does not work this week; she's off for Thanksgiving break. She has a second appointment with her therapist this week. She continues to do well.

In addition to counseling, I met with my priest last week for a spiritual check-in. Meeting with Father Michael has been an important component of my grieving process. Father Michael is a married Orthodox priest with five children and a background in chaplaincy. He's been very helpful to me.

In processing and talking to my wife, my mom, my brother, my kids, Fr. Michael, and a counselor, I am doing what I can to share my story and my emotions. It does help.

I have accepted that I am never going to be "healed." I do believe, however, I will heal better than today. I'm always going to have a big, raw, tender scar. I'm always going to have a shadow. I'm always going to have a small, black hole in my soul. I'm always going to have an empty feeling in my chest. I'm always going to have dreams of Cooper. I'm always going to wake up, take a deep breath, and realize yet again this is real.

This is better than the first week when I would wake up from a dead sleep with tears streaming from my eyes. Even in my sleep, I was crying.

Last Friday, Day 40, I took my jar of holy water and went into Cooper's living space in the house, and I blessed it in the name of the Father, Son, and Holy Spirit. Over and over, I sprinkled holy water with my right hand. On the doors, the halls, the rooms, the living spaces, the kitchen, the walls, the ceiling—all of it. It turned into a meditation as I chanted, "In the name of the Father, Son, and Holy Spirit... in the name of the Father, Son, and Holy Spirit... in the name of the Father, Son, and Holy Spirit..."

After that, I took what was left of the holy water, grabbed one of the dogs, Bear Bear, and we went for a drive. We drove out to the place where Cooper took his life. I don't know exactly where he was, but I have a general idea. Again, I prayed, poured the remaining holy water on the ground, and prayed for peace with the place, with nature.

Then I walked around with Bear Bear, took it all in, and prayed more. It was a nice morning. Sun up, clear skies, no wind, crisp. The birds were chattering their songs. Perhaps they knew. It is a beautiful, peaceful place, and I have a greater understanding of why Cooper chose this particular space in seeking peace for his soul.

It was hard being there, so we didn't stay long.

I had to stop at Home Depot on the way home to get a few things to fix a leaking toilet at the house. I got my parts, checked out, and as I was walking out with Bear Bear on his leash, a nice man, my age, stopped me to talk about dogs. He had had a Shih Tzu for 13 years before he died, and he was telling me how distraught he was when his dog died. He says, "I couldn't function, I couldn't sleep, it was the worst thing..."

I keep saying, grief is not a measuring contest. But if I am being fair, as I stood there and listened, I was feeling an emotional response on the inside. I was feeling like, "Dude, you have no idea..." I was not angry; it was more like I was perplexed. I was thinking, *Why am I standing here in Home Depot listening to this man tell me about his dog when my son died 40 days ago?* It was surreal, the experience felt like slow motion.

I kept smiling, listened, and I wished him a good day and moved on with my day. He meant no harm, but I thought it was interesting—we never know what people are carrying, do we?

Events like this make me more compassionate toward fellow travelers on this earth. I know we all suffer. This is part of the human condition. I wonder more about the people I meet these days. Are they suffering in this moment? Am I the smile, the kind heart, the listening third ear that buoys them for another day?

Perhaps it's all psychological, perhaps genuinely spiritual, but something did change on Day 40. Cooper's living area feels different to me now, more peaceful. I don't have the sense that his soul is hanging out, lingering, waiting for me to make him breakfast.

Yes, I was definitely more at peace Friday, especially toward the end of the day, as sundown came, 5:05 pm. And so ended Day 40.

Did Cooper find his way home? Yes, I think he did. As I was saying my morning prayers, calling upon God and the host of heaven to guide Cooper home, I genuinely had a sense of peace, that Cooper was in heaven. Then the wind chime, given as a gift in memory of Cooper and hanging on our front porch, chimed. My heart felt warm, and though my eyes were closed, things got brighter.

There were many people praying for Cooper's soul. They still are. It's incredible to me. I know the prayers helped, and I accept the grace offered. Why does it take tragedy to renew my belief in the kindness of people? Am I just seeing it all more clearly now, as my life moves in slower motion?

Just over 40 days ago was the last time we saw Cooper. We were at a tailgate party. My wife will never go to another tailgate party again during her lifetime. Period.

I made the decision yesterday to get back on the horse. I went to a tailgate party with many of the same people who were there the last time we saw Cooper. Though it was difficult, there was healing involved. A few people, Cooper's age, who were with him that last night, came over to me and shared their story, their pain, their grief. They, too, hurt. We hugged it out, talked it out, and shared some fun stories. It dawned on me as I was listening: they needed to vent and share with me. I was there for them.

It felt good being at the tailgate, but when I came home last night, I could tell I had overextended my emotional self.

I didn't sleep well.

The last time I went to a tailgate party, I came home, went to bed, and woke up to a different world. Scorched earth. Going to the tailgate party was fine, but I overlooked and forgot about the coming home and going to bed part. I slept in a different bed in the house last night and held a small cross necklace given to me by a former student; it was her grandmother's, and she gifted it to me.

I dreamed of being in a bookstore last night, and four dogs came in and came over to me. They were friendly toward me. There were three little white dogs, short-haired, Jack Russell Terriers, and one much smaller little brown Yorkshire Terrier. I was trying to read their dog tags and find their owner to return them. I couldn't read the tags, but I could read the prescription medicine tags the dogs had with them (I don't know why the dogs had prescription medicine receipts with them), and the phone number read, MAINE. Not a number, but just MAINE. Like that, in capitals.

You tell me.

I woke up this morning not feeling as good as I have been feeling over the last two weeks. Truth be told, it could be the emotions of last night, and/or the four Oktoberfest beers I consumed; just saying. Yes, I had a designated driver—my wife dropped me off and picked me up.

All of the kids are doing well. We are talking it out and staying in touch, and everyone is in the process of lining up counseling.

Friends and family, thank you for your prayers. We love you. You lift Cooper up, and you lift us up.

Many blessings.

~

boys in the basement
November 21, 2023

I grew up in Arizona, solidly middle class. Or maybe we were lower middle class, and I have more lofty memories than I ought to have. I'm not sure. I snow skied and slam danced. You tell me.

All things considered, our middle-class neighborhood was culturally diverse. My best friend throughout high school was South Korean. His mother was South Korean by birth, and his father was American. My friend's grandmother, directly from South Korea, lived with his family. It was three generations living together under one roof.

"Grandma" is pronounced "Halmeoni" in Korean. This is what we called my friend's grandmother, Halmeoni. Halmeoni spoke no English. None. Despite this, Halmeoni took on a grandmotherly role for me. When I visited my friend, which was often (he lived around the corner), Halmeoni always wanted to see my hands. She would look at my palms, rub them, and look up at me with her little old round face and smile warmly. I don't know if she was reading my palms, but I always assumed it was something like that. My friend never told me what she was doing; maybe he didn't know.

Halmeoni gave me a good feeling about my future. There was nothing in her smile that indicated an easy life, but I've always imagined a full and robust life based on what I read in her expressions while she was peering into my palms, or whatever it was she was doing.

I'm told that years later, on her deathbed, Halmeoni said my name, "Kelly." She said it a few times. I miss Halmeoni. She was a good grandmother to me.

Fast forward a few years. I am a young man now, a firefighter, and I am married with three small children—all boys at this point. Little Miss Sunshine (Grace), our daughter, was still just a twinkle in our eyes. We bought a house in a master-planned community in a cul-de-sac. Yes, I was still rolling solidly middle class. Or, you know, I am recalling life more loftily than I ought.

There were seven homes in the cul-de-sac. If you're into numbers, it's not a bad set.

Our immediate neighbors to the south were Orthodox Christians from Assyria. They fled their home country under extreme persecution. We immediately hit it off with this family. In fact, they called us family. They said, "If we have a problem and need help, our family, who lives many miles away, cannot help us. But you, you can help us. Therefore, you are now our family." It was a simple logic that made sense to me. Like my friend growing up, there were three generations living in this home. I had, once again, another grandma and grandpa. Grandpa Otto always wanted to shake my hand and stand in front of me, holding our handshake and smiling. This was our greeting. Like Halmeoni, my new grandparents spoke no English. We spent a lot of time with our neighbors eating and drinking, and the kids played together safely in the cul-de-sac.

Across the street in the cul-de-sac was a large Hispanic family. This family also had three generations living under one roof. The grandparents spoke little English. We were friends with this family and spent a lot of time in the cul-de-sac, drinking and smoking hookah with raspberry tobacco, courtesy of our Assyrian family. Their children were older, so our kids didn't spend as much time together.

These three families, in addition to our many Hispanic/Mexican family and friends, have influenced how I think about multigenerational living. They modeled it very well.

I've thought a lot about these families over the years. They were comfortable with their older children and parents living at home, perhaps indefinitely, under one roof. I've mentally compared and contrasted my observations of these families with white families. In white culture, which I am a part of, it's frowned upon for grown children to live at home. Grandparents rarely live at home; they are sent to nursing homes.

As I have labored in the workforce for many years and become a middle-aged man, I know how difficult it is to earn a living, support a family, build a life, and gain upward mobility. It's increasingly challenging to gain a foothold in life as a young person—even with a college degree and help from family.

By the time Cooper graduated from college in May 2022, we had moved to the Midwest to help care for my father-in-law. This left Cooper a few choices: 1) live with grandma and grandpa in Southern Arizona while job hunting, 2) live with mom and dad in the Midwest while job hunting, or 3) live with friends or brothers while job hunting. The bottom line was that we were no longer paying Cooper's rent.

As it happened, Cooper landed a job at the university and

moved from Southern Arizona to the Midwest, moving in with us. It was a quick, seamless, and smooth transition.

Serendipitously, I had spent the previous year remodeling our basement. The basement has hardwood flooring, a master bedroom with a walk-in closet, a full bath, a kitchen, an island, a workstation, a reading area, a living room, and a workout room. There is a large sliding glass door leading out to a patio area and the backyard. It is fully self-sustaining.

Cooper and Grace

Over the last year, as Cooper lived at home rent-free "in the basement," he was able to buy a new car, pay for it, and save a decent amount of money. We imagined Cooper would stay with us for one, maybe two years max. We simply told him he could stay as long as he wanted, but we figured it would be about a year. In fact, I came across a goal Cooper had written in his notes: "Goal: leave home by 2024."

As Cooper lived with us, my old family friends were on my mind. We were breaking with our cultural tradition to live together in a manner that comes more easily to other cultures.

It was nice having Cooper at home with us. We enjoyed his company. He did not spend a lot of time with us upstairs, but we did eat meals together on Sundays. Grandma and grandpa usually drove over and ate Sunday dinner with us, which was nice because Cooper was able to spend quality time with his grandfather before he died of Parkinson's in May.

(Incidentally, I do think Poppy Jack's death was one of the more recent triggers influencing Cooper's decision to take his own life. I will speak more about this in a future post.)

Remember, I have shared that Cooper had social anxiety. He stated in a text to a friend that his social anxiety sometimes caused him "pain" to talk with others. In another text, Cooper mentioned he saw a doctor, and the doctor suggested he might be depressed. On the heels of COVID-19, I know Cooper felt lonely and isolated because he told me so (November 2021).

Cooper, like all of us, wanted to connect with others. He wanted companionship. He wanted a girlfriend. But Cooper was not great at connecting and starting that first initial conversation. It was hard for him. For those who got through that initial social awkwardness and accepted Cooper as he was, he was deeply loved.

As I was going through Cooper's text messages looking for clues as to why he might have taken his life, and if it was preplanned (it was not), I came across a text exchange, several months old, that bothered me. It continues to bother me, which is why I am writing about it.

I don't believe the text exchange had anything to do with Cooper taking his life, but I don't think it helped either. It was another small lash for a young man who was struggling.

The text exchange is between Cooper and a girl he had just met. To keep it simple, the girl laughs Cooper off and ridicules him for living in his "parents' basement."

The text exchange hurts me on several levels.

First, being made fun of and ridiculed when I now know Cooper was hurting hurts me. But secondly, the exchange so easily glosses over what I have shared with my children regarding living together, two- or three-generations deep, based on how I have experienced life.

I have expressed to my children over the years that white culture, in regard to shipping their children off to college with the expectation they never come home, is limited and that we ought to be more open to adopting the healthy practices of multigenerational living found in different cultures.

I shared with Cooper over the last year that there is nothing wrong—nothing at all—with a young man living at home for a season of life to gain a financial foothold and make a better future for himself and his future family.

At 23 years of age, Cooper was judged by an arrogant young woman for living with his parents in their "basement." Never mind that it was his home too, that he had moved to a new town a year ago, and that the "basement" rivals modern apartments.

This mean girl piled on when she didn't need to.

I want to pause and reinforce: everybody we meet and come into contact with, make eye contact with, or have a conversation with may be deeply hurting. They may be alone and isolated, anxious and depressed.

Instead of piling on, can we build up?

Ridiculing a young man for living at home in his parents' basement is not okay. There should not be a stigma associated with boys in the basement, especially in this economy.

To the boys in the basement, I salute you. You're doing it right. Love your parents, save your money, get a better start in life, gain a foothold. You're doing your future family right.

Thank you for letting me get this off my chest.

just breathe and bruises

As we continue to process Cooper's death, navigate grief, and struggle our way toward, through, and around healing, I am leaning into music.

I've never been a huge music guy, but I am finding that music touches me in places other mediums do not. My soul, man.

I tear up listening to certain songs, but they are good tears. I lean my head back and show my whole face to Creation and let the tears stream down my cheeks.

I learned about lifting my head up and proudly showing my crying face while watching the documentary *The Work*.[1] I highly recommend this documentary. I wish there had something like this when I left the fire department; it would have been healing.

It would be healing now.

I do think sometimes men just need another man standing in front of them, staring them in the eyes, saying, "I got you. Let's go pick up the coins in the deep places."

Here are two more songs to add to my growing playlist:

- *Just Breathe,* Pearl Jam[2]
- *Bruises,* Lewis Capaldi[3]

Carse and Cooper

crane migration
November 25, 2023

I have a long-running habit of not drinking alcohol during the week, then, on Friday, I have a few beers. Saturday too. I'm glad binge drinking is now defined as five beers instead of three. Therefore, I don't binge drink on Friday.

Several months back, on a Friday night, my wife and I visited the local chophouse for happy hour. On this particular evening, the chophouse was running a special on a local craft beer. The beer was Migration Patterns, brewed by Crane Brewing in Raytown, Missouri.

Migration Patterns is a very hoppy IPA, the kind of beer that bites back. I love beer like this. In fact, Migration Patterns is easily one of my favorite IPAs.

I loved the beer, yes, but I also loved the name—Migration Patterns. Classic. It's right up there with Bent Nail, Czechmate, and Dipthong Cowboy. I have said over the years that I would like to get in on the beer naming game. I have ideas. For example, Urban Gestalt. This would be a locally sourced IPA brewed with hops and ingredients all grown and produced in urban gardens within a 50-mile radius. Think Detroit. You see? Urban Gestalt.

Anyway, this brief encounter with this very good craft beer led me to philosophically ponder crane migration patterns, like the real birds, which I knew nothing about. Of course, being the geek that I am, I read up on cranes and their migration patterns because, well, this is just how I am wired.

If you're old school and have watched *Northern Exposure*, you might imagine that I have touches of the philosopher radio host, Chris Stevens.

Turns out, sandhill cranes are actually quite fascinating. They migrate twice a year, with some flying 5,000 miles from Siberia to Mexico. These cranes average 200-300 miles per day, and with a good tailwind, they can cover 500 miles. The journey is dangerous for the cranes, mainly due to weather and hunters. Sandhill cranes can live 20-40 years. Impressive.

Consider this: sandhill cranes live 20-40 years and fly 5,000 miles twice per year. And do you know what they take for their journey? Their material possessions?

Nothing.

Compare and contrast. We, humans, are on this earth for 74-78 years on average. We don't migrate twice per year; as a general rule, we stay in only a few places over a lifetime. Despite this, we have many possessions. Many, many things.

For many years now, I have been nominally a minimalist. I at least have minimalist tendencies. When it comes to books, I fall short. I'm a book maximalist. Other than books, I simply don't have a lot of "toys," nor do I feel the need to have them. Boats, motorcycles, jet skis, etc.—all the man toys—I don't have them. I have never desired them.

I live pretty simply. I prefer a few high-quality things rather than many. Except books. I like lots of books.

My children, and in particular my boys, have adopted this minimalist philosophy in their own lives. I didn't teach it to them overtly; they absorbed my nuances by watching. I see it in their lives more clearly as they get older. They don't want things. They want to own few possessions and keep their living spaces tidy. It's a joy to observe this.

While none have done it yet, I have suggested to the boys that they travel the world with only a 30-liter backpack loaded with the essentials and just three pairs of ExOfficio underwear. This kind of minimalist travel is possible. My only admonition to them is that they must travel with another person or two. Jesus sent his disciples out two by two, not one by one.

Instead of taking his life, I wish Cooper had told the world to f**k off in no uncertain terms, cashed out, bought a 30-liter backpack and three pairs of chonies, and disappeared for a season or two of life—traversing the world. Or grounded himself in one culture, spending deep time learning their language and customs, becoming a better man as a result. I wish he had done as the Aboriginals do and just walked and not stopped walking until the demons were purged. *Salviture Ambulando.*

In the aftermath of Cooper's journey *al otro lado*, we have loosely gone through his things. For the most part, we have left everything in place, as if we're magically waiting for him to reappear. I think we're just not ready to say goodbye.

Cooper's clothes are washed, folded, and sitting in the laundry basket at the end of his bed. His wallet, watch, and necklace are on the kitchen island. Each morning, I lay my hand on them and try to soak up his essence.

His guitar is sitting here in the guitar stand, waiting. Oh, how I miss hearing him learn and develop on the guitar. I used to open the door a little wider when he was playing in the evenings and just listen. I now wish I had recorded him. I last remember him playing "Free Fallin'" by Tom Petty. Interesting now that I think about it.

What has been intriguing to me, in going through Cooper's things, is how few possessions he had. Given my minimalist tendencies, I should be happy about this. I am, but it also saddens me. I am not sure why.

Cooper was on this earth for 23 years. The Creation is better for his life.

This is what Cooper left behind:

- Mother, father, two brothers, one sister.
- Two grandmothers, one grandfather.
- Uncle (godfather), aunt, and cousin.
- One sister-in-law. Related family and friends.
- Snoopy, a 13-year-old Shih Tzu. Christmas gift, 2011.
- 2023 Honda Civic.

Technology:

- MacBook Pro— not much on it. A journal, a few notes, and a lot of math files from college.
- Gaming computer—Cooper built his own gaming computer when he was in middle school. *League of Legends* was Cooper's jam.
- Apple iPhone.
- Apple AirPods.

Accessories:

- Orient watch—brown leather band, gold bezel.
- Brown Hilfiger leather wallet.
- Driver's license, bank card, FAA student pilot's license, FAA drone pilot license, health insurance cards.
- Necklaces:
  - Sterling silver Figaro necklace.
  - Carpe Diem sterling silver necklace, Maritime Supply Company. Gift from me.
  - St. Christopher necklace—from Grandma Kathy.

Personal Items:

- Columbia, University of Arizona embroidered 19-liter backpack—from the college days.
- Cessna Pilot's backpack—filled with flight information, 200 logged hours.
- Ibanez Performance Acoustic Guitar—Natural, with stand.
- Seven books: *Dune; Meditations; Trinity; Endure; Boys NIV Bible: The Ultimate Manual; Good Poems for Hard Times; Phi Delta Theta Manual.*

Workout Equipment:

- 100 lb. Everlast heavy bag.
- Krav Maga combat gloves (for heavy bag work).
- Pull-up bar.
- Wood gymnastic rings.
- 2, 35 lb. kettlebells.
- 2, 30 lb. dumbbells.
- 2, 20 lb. dumbbells.
- 20 lb. Rep Fitness medicine ball.
- 50-125 lb. Rep Fitness sandbag.
- Jump rope.

- Resistance bands.
- Yoga mat.
- GymBoss timer.
- Jujitsu gi.
- Scale.
- Soccer ball, soccer cleats.

Other Items:

- Ping golf clubs, in trunk of car—from Grandpa James.
- Floating tube—back of car, for the local lake.
- Ray-Ban sunglasses—aviator style.
- Hydro Flask 32 oz.
- Hardshell travel suitcase, carry-on size.

Clothing:

- Various, but minimal. Cooper was fond of Carhartt, Lululemon, Patagonia, Vans, and North Face brands.
- Rosary—given to Cooper as a gift from Grandma Kathy. This was buried with Cooper, in his hands.
- Outdoor Research 600 down fill hooded jacket.
- Three hats—University of Arizona, North Face, Life is Good.
- Oboz hiking boots.
- Three Carhartt beanies.

Memorabilia:

- Mexican prayer candle—Holy Spirit.
- Framed diploma, natural oak—University of Arizona, May 2022, BS Aerospace Engineering.
- Cap and gown, two stoles—College of Engineering, Phi Delta Theta.

- Phi Delta Theta picture and certificate of membership.
- Change jar—1/4 full, mostly foreign coins.
- A small stack of graduation and 21st birthday cards in the nightstand next to bed.
- Nesting dolls.
- Two Snoopy stuffed animals.
- University of Arizona queen-size fleece.
- Two small stretched canvas prints—one of the ocean, lots of orange, and one of the city, lots of purple.
- 8 x 10 painting of a Shih Tzu, looks exactly like Snoopy.

About a year ago, I was working with a very intelligent team developing an online course for volunteer firefighters. The team leader would frequently say, "I have questions..." She said this from a standpoint of curiosity.

I continue to grieve well, I think. But I have questions. So many questions. Most of which will go unanswered. I simply don't understand.

Beyond my questions, it's perplexing to me how lightly Cooper treaded this earth. I am happy for his gentle, quiet spirit and light footprint.

Back to that hoppy beer, Migration Patterns.

Like a sandhill crane, Cooper has migrated, taking nothing with him for the journey and leaving few possessions behind. Well, to be fair, he left on his journey wearing the same suit he graduated in, his dog's collar and a rosary in his hands, and letters written to him by family.

Though he lived quietly and gently, what Cooper did leave behind, the etching upon our hearts, is impressive.

crippin

November 28, 2023

The day before Thanksgiving, the girls (my wife and daughter) and I drove out to the cemetery to be present with our son, pray for him, and simply pay our respects and honor him. Because Poppy Jack (grandpa) is literally right next to Cooper, we did the same for him.

Cooper and Poppy Jack

We were also able to stand over our future burial plots and take a deep breath. Surreal.

I feel a great sense of peace at the cemetery. We are first a sensing and feeling people, then a thinking people. I feel peace in my chest when I visit my son's final resting place, my future resting place, my wife's future resting place. No thought, just felt peace. Warmth. I sense you, thin space; I feel you.

The skies were clear, sprinkled with clouds, the wind calm, the temperature in the 50s. A perfect Arizona day... in the Midwest! If you're from Arizona, you know of what I preach.

The cemetery is well kept. There are many trees, the grass is mowed nicely, and the surroundings are natural Midwest grasses and trees. It's quiet, except for the low hum of highway. The sun comes through the trees at the right angles, and the birds and bugs fly about.

I am glad we made the decision to bury Cooper next to his grandfather in this place. I'm also glad I know where I will come to rest.

I used to be good friends with an Anglican priest, Kyle. Kyle baptized our daughter in Asheville, North Carolina. In the lake, Lake Powhatan, by full immersion. All of our children—one, two, three, four—were baptized in the Anglican church. (We're no longer Anglicans, but that's a different blog post...)

Kyle moved to the South years ago, and through distance and time, our friendship has waned. I still count Kyle as a friend; we just don't communicate often. I'm one of those people who holds time. I have certain friends, a small group, whom I haven't seen in 20 years, and if I were to see them today, we would pick right back up where we left off. This holds true for Kyle.

I remember attending an *If You Were Mine* adoption conference with Kyle in Texas. After a day of conferencing, we went to a local pub and were waxing philosophical about life. A conversation about "home" came up. Kyle asked me, "Where do you consider your home, Kelly?" It was an interesting question.

I couldn't answer the question, so Kyle asked me in a different way, "Where do you want to be buried when you die?" I said I really didn't know. He said, "When you can answer that question, then you will know where your home is." Sage wisdom; I guess that's why he's a priest.

I was not born in the Midwest, but my wife was. We moved to the Midwest in 2020 to help care for her father, whose health was failing due to Parkinson's disease.

I thought when we moved to Montana from Arizona, that Montana was my final "home," that there would be no more moves, that it would be the place I was buried. I really believed that. I had visions of becoming a bearded old man with dogs in the front seat of my 1970 wood-paneled Grand Wagoneer, living and tinkering about the mountains.

Where's my home now? The Midwest. I had a premonition when we moved to the Midwest that this would be my final place, my home, the place where I was buried. I had no idea it would involve the loss of my youngest son, but here we are.

Anyway, last week, after praying and talking with Cooper and Poppy, we walked around the cemetery looking at headstones. We have not yet purchased a headstone for Cooper. As we walked about, we were looking for ideas and inspiration. As I have already mentioned, I am a minimalist. My wife is too, to a lesser degree.

If I were to go back in my life 20 years, I would tell you that death scared me. I disliked funerals, cemeteries, hospice, all manner and talk of death. I know why this is. When I was young, in 4th grade, a good friend was killed by a train. Later, in my early teens, my best friend was electrocuted. Death introduced itself too early into my life in traumatic ways. It scared me.

I don't know what's happened over the years as I've aged—maybe it's just maturity, maybe 25 years of firefighting and coming face to face with death pretty frequently—but I no longer fear death.

"Yea, though I walk through the valley of the shadow of death, I will fear no evil, for you are with me; your rod and your staff, they comfort me." I wish I could say God is the reason I no longer fear death, as if I have a profound belief in the beauty of the afterlife in heaven. Maybe. It's probably more the case that I am jaded and death has simply lost its sting.

It was weird how easily we walked around this cemetery, quietly talking and looking for headstone ideas. My wife and I are in agreement: we are looking for something simple, dignified, and unique. The three of us walked and talked and respectfully spent time with the dead. How interesting is my life becoming? Why?

You contracted in on yourself, Cooper; are you now an expanding supernova star spilling into my, our, life?

It was a good day.

The next day, Thanksgiving, we bucked tradition and had cheeseburgers on the Blackstone with seven-layer dip, deviled eggs, and baked beans. Simple. The boys did not fly in for Thanksgiving, but they will come for Christmas. Grandma came over and ate with us. Me and the three ladies. Winning.

Was Thanksgiving a hard day? Yes. What I am learning in child loss is that as a father, I know I have a child missing. It's palpable, not as an added weight, but as a negation, an emptiness, a vacuum. I have an internal homing beacon that is always aware of and tracking my kids in the back of my mind, night and day. My beacon knows Cooper is not here; there's a negative space.

This emptiness hurts, and I think it's what they call grief.

Recently, I came across two pictures of sculptures on the internets (I am purposely writing 'internets' in plural; give it time, you will learn to appreciate my humor). These sculptures help describe how I am sometimes feeling. It's hard for me to put into words how I feel because I have new emotions I have never experienced before. These emotions are complex and interwoven, and they ebb and flow. It's a real treat, let me tell you.

Albert György, Mélancolie, 2012, by art_inthecity, CC 2.0, Wikimedia Commons

Melancholy,[1] is a sculpture created by Albert György, located in Lake Geneva, Switzerland. This sculpture really sums up deep, painful grief and loss very well. Not as much today, but I have definitely been this man following Cooper's death.

Alessandroni Grave,[2] is a monument in Verano Monumental Cemetery, Rome, Italy, and it also depicts grief and loss very well.

Hooded sorrow, Verano Cemetery, Rome, 2009, by Hans, D., CC 2.0, Wikimedia Commons

As I pick my head up and look around me, I see that I am not the only one experiencing these complex emotions. My wife is,

Cooper's brothers are, his sister, his grandparents, his uncle, related family, his close friends, and close family friends, all are. I'm simply the writer here, sharing my grief in the hopes of finding some healing. I am aware we all hurt, and I am not alone. Further, I know there are other parents who have lost children, and they hurt too.

This is a tough gang to be in. The beat-in leaves a mark. Crippin.

~

here i am
December 1, 2023

People grieve in different ways and at different paces. This is a recurring message in my various readings of grief literature. I understand this.

However, I still don't know if I am doing it right. I feel okay, so maybe my array of practices is right for me. Time will tell. I will just keep putting one foot in front of the other.

One of my early approaches in navigating my traumatic grief was to do the best I could to figure out why Cooper took his life. I wanted answers. I wanted to make sense of his death where I was able to do so. To me, this felt like honoring Cooper. I feel like if I just shrug my shoulders and don't ask questions, it's dishonorable. I don't want to live like that; it's not who I am.

Full geek mode is part of my identity. I know, I know—it's hard to get past my rugged good looks to see my hidden geek, but it's there (more humor, hang in there with me).

A few weeks after Cooper died, when I could breathe and stand, thanks be to the grace of compassionate friends, I downloaded an application[1] to my MacBook that allowed me to create timelines. I wanted to create a timeline. What I wanted to know in creating the timeline was whether there were red flags over the years that we missed, which, when seen collectively, would make more sense of this tragedy. The short answer is yes, to some degree, but every little bit helps when you are a grieving father.

A few days after Cooper's death, one of my wife's coworkers arrived at the door with snacks and food. I greeted her, and she said with tears in her eyes, "I can't even imagine." Her tears made me tear up. But what she expressed is true. Losing a child is the most unimaginable event that's happened in my life. I don't ask myself this question often, but I have asked it: "Why us? Why are we called to endure the unendurable?"

The only people who know are those who know. Trust me, you don't want to know.

I created a timeline going back to Cooper's sophomore year of high school, which is where we first had at least a yellow flag, if not a red one.

Following Cooper's death, somehow, I was able to gain access to his iPhone without his passcode. It's weird because, while I didn't have his passcode, I did have his laptop. Miraculously, my oldest son was able to use the gaming computer Cooper built to find a few older passwords and then crack the password to Cooper's MacBook.

With access to Cooper's MacBook and iPhone, we were able to reset his iPhone. The iPhone did erase most everything on it when it reset, but it did retain text messages going back to January 2020. I was also able to get into Cooper's email, which he had since 5th grade—and he never deleted anything! Yep, 7,000 promotional emails, all still there...

I wasn't going through these efforts because I am nosy. In fact, I value privacy greatly. To wit, there are some things I came across that I have not shared with my wife. She doesn't need to know, nor do others. I was going through this effort because I wanted to know why my son took his life.

You must understand, for us, this was completely unexpected. In one morning, a micro-atomic bomb was dropped on our house, and our hearts were shattered, I think maybe even literally. Scorched earth. Ripples of emotional and spiritual pain traveling in shock waves to family and friends.

I've read everything I could read, and where it was applicable to Cooper's mental health, I added that information to the timeline. This exercise didn't solve the mystery of the Unfolding, but it did fill in many missing gaps. As I have mentioned before, I now have a charcoal sketch, but not a complete picture.

For example, one of Cooper's very good friends, a best friend, admirably, honorably, and responsibly called him out for certain behavior during his junior year of college, telling Cooper directly that his behavior was not okay and that, as his friend, he was concerned. This friend stood by Cooper's side and helped him while courageously telling him things were not okay. This is an event that helps me, as a grieving father, sketch a fuller picture.

After I did the timeline exercise, I created two mind maps. The first mind map was writing "general considerations" for why Cooper might have taken his life. For this exercise, I just let my imagination flow and allowed that no ideas were off limits. I wanted to generate thoughts and many of them. I knew I could come back at a later time and apply more diligence to the mind mapping. This was a broad mind map, like a lighthouse shining light all around.

The second mind map I created was mapping "recent triggers." This was a flashlight exercise. I was striving to think more specifically about recent triggers that may have led to Cooper's death. For example, Cooper's grandfather died in May 2023, and perhaps it was harder on him than he expressed. I think this is true, and I view this as a recent trigger that, among other triggers, cascaded into a mental health crisis.

Importantly, as I was thinking through these exercises, I was having a lot of dialogue with my wife about my thoughts. We were processing together. She helped review the timeline and the mind maps, and we talked through them together.

As an example, I had forgotten that Cooper had a fairly serious concussion while playing high school soccer during his senior year. We added this to the timeline. Maybe it was a factor at play, maybe not, but it's an example of drawing out a fuller picture.

Another exercise I did was write a list of questions. I knew in writing most of the questions that I was not going to get an answer, but I still wanted to write the questions. I allowed myself to just ask questions, knowing there would be no answers forthcoming. But I did put the questions out there into the Universe.

Creating a timeline and thinking through two mind maps, general considerations and recent triggers, reading through Cooper's emails, texts, and social media, and writing down a list of questions helped me to fill in some gaps that were missing. It's provided me with a sense of conducting due diligence as a father to understand my son's death. This was important to me.

This is how I was grieving in the early weeks—sense-making. Or maybe this was flat-out dissociation, I don't know. I believe I was present in the work, but I did lose a sense of time.

After these exercises, I reached out to a few of Cooper's friends to talk. Firstly, I know Cooper's death has impacted many of his friends; it's hard on them. They say one suicide affects, on average, 135 people. I believe it. It's so easy for me in my grief to drop my head, go inward, and zone the world out. In fact, I find myself walking with my head down a lot these days, lost in my thoughts.

I believe that it's okay that I go inward and spend time caring for myself and thinking, but I also believe it's important to pick my head up and look around at the people around me. How are they doing? In calling a few of Cooper's friends, I wanted to share in their grief with them. They are damn good kids.

I think grief is easier when we circle the wagons together. A thousand million threads bind us, and we need each other in grief. John Donne, my man JD, has it right: no man is an island, entire unto himself.[2] As I often say, the smallest individual unit in the kingdom of God is two, not one.

But I had questions for Cooper's friends too. Did they see anything that caused them concern? Now that they look back, is there anything that stands out to them, that makes more sense in retrospect? In talking with these friends, there was not much new added to help make sense of his death.

Finally, we are still waiting for the results from the autopsy and toxicology reports. Maybe more information is forthcoming, or maybe nothing. I don't know. Unless my dad radar is completely broken, I simply don't see anything profound coming up on these reports. Would it change anything? No. But might it help make more sense of things? Yes. Is this important? To me, yes.

Cooper didn't leave us a note, and there is no evidence I can find that this was preplanned. So what happened?

Can you see my theme here? The unanswered questions haunt me, and part of my grieving process is to answer what I am able to reasonably answer.

I am using this blog post to set up a few future blog posts. Below are topics I intend to draw out and discuss at length. I want to wax on how these topics influence suicide in society.

- Technology/screen time and brain development—in particular, the prefrontal cortex and its potential underdevelopment in digital natives.
- Loneliness, isolation, and shame—this is a dangerous three-headed dragon.
- Social media, dopamine hits, fried nervous systems at a young age, measuring up, and the perceived existential threat of not belonging to the tribe.
- Global events presenting as local and amplified by social media and emotional contagion—e.g., Ukraine-Russia, Israel-Gaza, and the unique stress this causes on the human psyche.
- The war on boys, young men, and "toxic masculinity" narratives; death by a thousand lashes.
- Drugs, alcohol, and college culture—particularly psychedelics, and the academy's break from objective reality.
- Elected officials acting like petulant children instead of behaving as authentic leaders.
- Being introverted in an extroverted society; lack of silence in a noisy world.
- No rites of passage for our young and the impact this might have.
- Mental health—depression, anxiety; these are global pandemics.
- Rogue/extractive capitalism (as opposed to generative economies), the military-industrial-complex, consumerism/consumption, and the disconnect between evolutionary-biological human development and the demands of the modern workplace.

- The impact COVID-19 had/has on mental health—especially the specific messaging of "social distancing and isolation" for those already socially challenged and prone to isolation.
- Suicide statistics—In the United States, ~50,000 in 2022, one every 11 minutes, ~80% men, ~76% white, and the second leading cause of death for those aged 10-24.

Let me end with this today. Sadly, I believe Cooper's suicide is just the tip of the iceberg. There have already been too many suicides, and my fear is there are going to be many, many more —for a variety of reasons. As I was speaking to the memorial stone representative a few days ago, he shared that they have already seen a marked increase in suicides. This is called "ground truth."

I want to carefully and compassionately start unpacking why suicide among white men and Native American men is so high and what we can do about it.

The first thing I would say is we need to stop disparaging men for being men. Period. The war on boys must stop.

If you have young men in your life—heck, any man—look them in the eyes today and tell them you love them and appreciate them and that you are glad they exist.

Ladies, you are loved. My advocacy for men is not a negation of women. I am just sensing very deeply that part of my mission moving forward is going to be advocating for young men and building them up. Young men are hurting very badly, and they need our help.

Here I am, Lord. Send me.

red fox

In deep sorrow and grief, we lose track of time, don't we? It was October, now it's December. My sense of time, in grief, is disrupted. I lack flow; I move in starts and stops. My wife comes home from work and asks, "What did you do today?" and I don't have a ready answer for her. I know I did many things, had many thoughts, but I am hard-pressed to remember the details. She understands.

My daily ritual of leaving the back door cracked open has changed. It's now too cold to leave the door cracked all day, so I briefly open it in the morning and say, "Good morning, Cooper. I love you. You're always welcome here. Come on in, Boy, or go out, either way..." Then I shut the door. After that, I place my hands on his wallet, necklace, and watch, still sitting on the kitchen island, and I breathe deep and soak up his essence. I say "I love you" again. Then I repeat this ritual in the evening and leave a light on for him. Above the light on the end table, just to the left, is a wooden cross hung on the wall, illuminated by the lone light in the room.

A very peculiar thing has happened since I started my new ritual. About two weeks ago, I opened the back door in the morning, and a bright red fox, with a clean and shiny coat, pointy nose, and fluffy tail, ran out from underneath the porch directly beneath the back door. One morning, it stopped and looked at me, both of us frozen. I was scanning its face, looking for clues. I could see its intelligence. A red fox, it seems, has taken up residence under the porch, right underneath the back door.

I wonder about this. Were we living in a magical world, where rationality was subdued and the spiritual was made larger and given more space in our lives, what are the chances this fox is Cooper, or some spiritual reflection of him? I have little trouble imagining the cardinals flying around my backyard are dear loved ones, so why not a red fox?

Why does my rational mind so quickly dismiss my spiritual wonder? I have questions.

We have moved the makeshift prayer altar from the dining room table to a smaller table in our living room. Actually, it's a library. (Do you remember I explained I am a book maximalist?) I'm still lighting a daily candle and praying for Cooper. My prayer remains simple: peace, happiness, love, and safety for Cooper's eternal soul. I pray beyond Cooper, of course, to include the healing of family and friends, most especially my wife.

What's spiritually interesting to me is that I spend at least a fair amount of my time in prayer these days praying for dear loved ones already departed from this life on earth. Early after Cooper's death, I was asking for the prayers of my departed loved ones and the saints to watch over and guide Cooper. Now, I pray for my deceased loved ones in a way I have not done before. This is a new aspect of prayer for me, opening up new dimensions in my spiritual life I have previously not explored.

We're approaching two months since Cooper died. I'm doing okay. Not bad, probably not great. I have my moments, both good and bad, and I accept them.

Just this week, I have been going through scrapbooks of Cooper that my wife has made and kept over the years. I cried as I was slowly flipping through the pages, not so much for the loss of Cooper, yes, that too, but for the love and care my wife has put into these albums. She has captured his life since birth in these beautiful books, and my heart breaks for her. The love my wife has for her children is so rich and deep and loving, I know she is crushed.

I am a father who deeply loved his son, and I am crushed, but I know the loss of Cooper is on another order of magnitude for my wife. A mother losing her child is, I think, the most tragic event that could happen to a mother.

I just finished reading *Bearing the Unbearable: Love, Loss, and the Heartbreaking Path of Grief*[1] by Joanne Cacciatore. It's a very good book. If I had to summarize, and using my own words and writing from memory, I would write:

> Our society does not do grief well. Everybody, our culture, wants those grieving to hurry up and get back to their old, normal selves. Problematically, when you lose a child (or dear loved one), there is no return to the old self. That person is gone. If the people around us rush us, make us hurry up in our grieving—mostly because our grief makes them uncomfortable—it causes more problems down the road. No, the only way out is through. We must learn to sit with, be with, the incredible empty loss and pain of losing our dear child. Grieving takes the time it takes; it must be done in a healthy way that suits the griever, and it's likely grieving and sorrow never actually

leave, but rather our capacity to cope and be with, sit with, the pain, grows. As we come to terms with our grief and do the work, we may be able to channel our grief and help others.

Imagine the biggest, meanest monster you can bring to mind. Grief is walking up to the monster, standing toe to toe with it, looking it in the eyes, and not blinking. There's great fear, the body quivers, and you don't know how this is going to turn out. You don't want to fight the monster, muscle up on it; you just want the monster to know, you're not going anywhere and you will stand your ground. You fear not.

It is a rather unfortunate paradox that I can only now see the pain of others more clearly, even feel it in my bones, because I know it.

Does this make me more human?

Two months ago, I (we) got hit by a freight train. My spirit, mind, and body are still broken and deeply bruised. I am healing, but slowly. I am being patient and gentle with my healing. I don't want to be sitting in a counselor's office ten years from now because I didn't do the deep work necessary to properly grieve the death of my son.

Imagine with me if you will: rather than Western medicine, I am sitting in a cave in the side of a Himalayan mountain with a Nepalese family, and they are caring for me in the traditional manner. This is a place where there is no doctor. I drink herbal tea with yak's milk, and my bones are mended by herbal remedies. Since body and soul are in substantial union, the mending of my body mends my soul. Let's call this Seven Years in ~~Tibet~~ the Midwest. I am not rushing this. If I literally have to go live in a cave to heal, it's what I will do.

Another way of saying this is, nobody is going to make me rush getting over my son's death. I'm going to marinate in it until my sinews are stained in his memories. I want to be able to close my eyes and etch the lines of his face by memory. I want to recite the scriptures by heart, by memory, and in this case, my holy book is Cooper.

I made it out to have a few craft beers with a dear friend last night. She, too, knows grief. I enjoyed very much that my friend wanted to talk about Cooper and to hear of my grief and sorrow. She was not afraid to engage in the uncomfortable conversation that sends most people running for the hills.

I like it when people can stand in the center of the fire with me and talk about Cooper. As a former firefighter, standing in the center of the fire has meaning to me. Oriah (Mountain Dreamer) would call this *The Invitation*.[2] Or, of the 100 men in my life, only one is a warrior who makes the difference in standing with me to navigate and explore the unseen, healing the wounds nobody can see.

Let's face it squarely: most of society is very scared of death and dying, and I understand this... up to a point. But I think, too, genuine spiritual maturity requires that, over time, we become more open and accepting of death, on account of the faith we hold. No?

I still talk to my mom almost every day, and we both agree: death does not scare us. We're not looking forward to dying, but the sting is gone. We have a great belief we will see our loved ones again, especially dear Cooper.

There are worse things than death, I know, because I am living it. I have always prayed to God over these many years, "God, if you ever think you need one of my kids, no, take me." All day long, every parent knows this.

I wish I could wrestle God, like Jacob. I know I would get beat, but I would like one night of going toe to toe with God. He would certainly feel me.

That's the thing with living a long life: you will experience a lot of suffering.

As the years go by and the sweet bliss of raising my family fades into the background, suffering seems to press into my life more forcefully, more frequently, and finds more of the open pores of my soul.

I'm not depressed. I smile, I laugh, and I see color in my life; bright red foxes, for example. I have hope for my future, and I enjoy living.

But right now, I am more partial to healing with my Nepalese family and drinking tea with yak's milk. This is where I am at.

Yes, I have questions. I am starting to have ideas too...

riptide

Cooper James was born in the month of June, 2000. Historically, June is an interesting month. Here are a few examples:

- June, 1933: FDR takes the US off the gold standard.
- June, 1981: The first scientific report on AIDS is published.
- June, 1991: Mikhail Gorbachev receives a Nobel Peace Prize.
- June, 2013: The Guardian newspaper publishes the first NSA leaked documents by Edward Snowden.

Cooper was born in Arizona. Cooper is my wife's third child, and he slipped right on out of that dilated cervix. Really, he kind of did. It was a relatively "easy" delivery, especially compared to our firstborn, which turned into an emergency C-section and was very hard on my wife and oldest son.

I state my wife had an "easy" delivery from the cheap seats, Monday morning quarterbacking, and backseat driving. As for my part in the delivery, I almost passed out. The doctor asked me if I wanted to cut the umbilical cord, and I did. After cutting the cord, I turned three shades of green and lay down in a recliner, all the way back, horizontal. Were it not for that recliner, I would have been lights out. Yeah, big, bad paramedic-firefighter I was...

Thanks be to God, Cooper was born healthy. He measured in the 5th percentile for weight and 10th percentile for height. He was small. Cooper's next older brother, two years older, was also born in the lower percentiles for height and weight. What was perplexing about this is that nobody in our family is small in stature. We're all average height and weight, even tall.

We had a wonderful pediatrician, and he did a work-up on Cooper and his brother. The diagnosis? Constitutional delay. Which meant the boys would grow to average height and weight, but it would be delayed. And that's what happened. Cooper was 5'11" and 180 pounds the day he died. Now, to be fair, Cooper worked really hard to gain weight. He ate a lot and worked out hard for his gains. He earned all 180 lbs., which is a testament to his tenacity.

Cooper's smallness was never a concern for me because I knew one day he would grow. We used to joke with Cooper in good nature, "Cooper, you can't have it all. You're kind, smart, loving, and good-looking. Do you really think God was going to give you the 100% package and give you height too? Come on, man. That just wouldn't be fair. Let's give the ladies a fighting chance..."

It never dawned on me that Cooper's smaller stature up until late high school may have bothered him. But it did. Cooper was up in Montana visiting over a college break, and we were eating ramen at a local restaurant. He said something I still remember that's just one of the many things I think about now. He said, and I am paraphrasing, "I know I am regular size now, but I still feel like I am small in my mind." In this conversation, Cooper intimated, in no uncertain terms, that it always kind of bothered him that he was smaller than his peers growing up.

I have vivid memories of Cooper playing soccer, beginning in 1st grade and through his senior year of high school on the varsity team. Cooper was almost always the smallest player on the field, but he balled, man. He really was a very good soccer player. He worked and played hard, battled the bigger players, and his size never seemed to limit him. I know his teammates and friends would corroborate this. He was a solid, starting member of the varsity team; a center midfielder.

Cooper loved soccer. It was one of his passions. This past September, Cooper flew to Miami, FL, with two coworkers to watch Messi play, but unfortunately, after the tickets were bought, Messi bailed on the game. They still went and watched the game, sans Messi. Sadly, this trip was a recent trigger for Cooper. Not because he didn't have fun—to the contrary. Cooper came home and, through tears, stated he had forgotten how much fun it was to be with friends and hanging out. My wife and I both identify this trip to Florida as a recent trigger among several others. It was good that he went, but it stirred up a lot of emotion for him.

There is one time, though, where Cooper's stature did matter, and it's another reflection for me that gives me pause.

When we lived in Southern Arizona, San Diego, California, was our quick escape vacation destination. It's a 5.5-hour drive, and before you know it, your toes are wiggling in the sand on the beach. You look out at the vast ocean and see no end. You feel the ocean breeze on your body, take a deep breath and fill your lungs full with salty air, and you feel your shoulders drop and the stress release. San Diego was our regular family vacation go-to. We love SD.

Our favorite place to stay in Southern California (SoCal) was in a beach cottage in La Jolla. We walked to Windansea Beach and spent the day in the surf and sand, and everyone was happy. Given the option of SeaWorld, Legoland, or the beach, the kids chose the beach every time.

Cooper, Grace, Carse, CJ, Windansea Beach, La Jolla, CA

One of the activities that the boys and I were fond of was wave crashing. We would simply stand in the surf, and as the waves were about to crash, we would dive into them at the base and come up and out on the other side. It was fun, and we would spend hours crashing waves.

On one particular day, the tide was in, it was a high tide day, and the wind was up. This meant very big waves. If I recall, they were in the neighborhood of six feet. As we were crashing waves on this big wave day, I looked over and saw Cooper starting to get caught up in waves too big for him. I swam over to him, grabbed him, and swam back to shore with him. Afterward, I told Cooper, "You're out. The waves are too big." And they were, especially for his stature. He was not happy; he wanted to hang in there with his brothers.

Academically and intellectually, not many could hang with Cooper. Cooper did not flaunt his intellect; in fact, you would never know he was gifted. Physically, growing up, however, Cooper had to work harder than his peers for many years to play at the same level. I wonder now how this manifested in his psyche.

Shortly after I removed Cooper from the ocean, Carse bailed. A few waves later, CJ and I tapped out. It was simply too rough, and the waves were too big.

This was 2008. In 2015, I retired from the fire department, and I was not doing well. I had stress injury from 25 years of slow grind, and it took me several months to find my balance and regain equilibrium. Lucky for me, I fell in with the Buddhists and took up meditation, and it was healing for me.

I must say, it never bothered me that I was meditating with the Buddhists in light of my Christian faith. I reasoned then, and I still do today, that God's love is big. I believed then, as I do now, there's absolutely nothing I can do that will separate me from the love of God, even if I willfully tried. I believed then that Jesus was so deep in the marrow of my bones that I was not even entirely myself, but at least in part, Jesus.

Spending time with the Buddhists was good for me, healing, and I have zero regrets. I would do it all over again.

In October of 2015, I ended up at a silent meditation retreat at Spirit Rock, an active Buddhist monastery. I took noble vows of silence and spent quiet time in meditation day and night for a week. It was life-changing.

It's the first time I saw an enlightened person. I was sitting in silence, having lunch, and gazing out the window. As I gazed, a hundred yards out, a Buddhist nun walked up a tree-lined path. She wore a maroon robe, had a shaved head, and she was glowing, smiling ear to ear, all by herself. A radiance surrounded her, like a golden orbit. She walked against a backdrop of tall trees, the tops of which swayed in the wind, or perhaps they were bowing—I don't know. I was stunned.

On night four, I had a dream. I wrote the dream in my journal, June 26th, 2015. I wrote exactly this:

Day 5

> Had a dream last night that Cooper was caught in a riptide and I dove in and swam out to him and was helping keep his head up and swim. I think Cooper could be drowning in his perfectionism and trying to keep up; he needs my help.

The dream reminded me of our big wave day in La Jolla. I never shared this dream with Cooper because it scared me—because in the dream, I was never sure if I kept Cooper's head up and saved him.

I did not.

Three to four weeks before Cooper died, before he took his own life (I hate saying and writing this, but I feel that it's important I do so), I asked Cooper if he wanted to go for a walk with me. As we were walking through the neighborhood in silence for a long time—because Cooper was not much of a conversationalist—I suddenly asked him, "Do you know how to get out of a riptide?" He said, "Yeah." I said, "Then tell me." Cooper shared correctly that you don't fight the current, but swim parallel to the shore and then angle in or come in when you're out of the rip. I asked

Cooper, "Does that have any meaning to you?" He said, jokingly, "No, but I bet you can figure something out on how it does."

He was right, of course. I wax too philosophical sometimes. A lot of times. Yeah, most of the time.

Thing is, now that Cooper is not here, and on account of what happened, I am convinced part of the reason he took his life is that he was drowning in his perfectionism, swimming against the rip, rather than parallel to the shore, and then swimming in.

Life is uncanny. Four months ago, I flew out to Arizona to be with Carse and spend a few days. We went out one night and lit it up. Pizza and beer led to playing pool and drinking beer, which led to karaoke and drinking more beer and smoking cigarettes, and before I knew it, we were walking home at 4 a.m., very drunk. At the karaoke bar, in the wee hours, we were sitting at a table with a group of pilots in training. This was a good group, and we were having fun. One of the pilots leaned over and confided in me that she had failed a particular flight maneuver that day, and she was being particularly hard on herself, abusing herself with alcohol, as was I. I listened patiently. Thinking of my son Cooper, also a pilot in training, I asked, "Are you a perfectionist?" She looked at me stunned, deer-in-the-headlights stunned, like I had just seen into her soul. Yes, she said slowly.

I gave the only advice I could give in the moment. I said, "Smile, don't take yourself too seriously, and don't swim against the rip."

Where am I? I'm right here. What time is it? It's right now.

made it better

Many years ago, I attended one of those generic leadership seminars. I honestly cannot, for the life of me, remember the name of the event. It was held at the local indoor sports arena. It was a packed event with literally thousands of attendees. Of particular interest to me was speaker Dr. John C. Maxwell. He is the reason I attended the event—I wanted to hear him speak.

Surprisingly, however, it was an unknown military speaker who had the greatest impact on me. I love being surprised by the positive when I least expect it.

One time, my flight was delayed going through Dallas Fort Worth Airport—I know what you're thinking, *that's weird, flight delays rarely happen at DFW*—and I was sitting in those little airport seats, zoning out and people-watching. Unexpectedly, two young children, about five years old, who did not know each other, started the mirror game. You know, one person does some type of body movement, and then the other person mirrors it or makes something up. The spontaneity of their interaction and the innocence touched me. There was not a face in that section that wasn't wearing a smile ear to ear watching these kids. Serendipitous magic, right there.

Like this, the military leader surprised me. He was not all "Hoorah!" beating his chest. He was deep, philosophical, intelligent—and a good orator. He gave an exceptionally good presentation, and I remember taking a lot of notes. Sadly, I don't recall this leader's name today, but by now, if you have been following my writing, you know we're not going to let details ruin a good story.

The key concept this leader presented was what he called "move it to the right." It's what I remember some twenty years later. He was talking about geopolitical, military conflict in the world and how, at least historically, the US military strived to move conflict to the right and de-escalate it. He explained that there were steps along the way, on a continuum, where a conflict could be de-escalated and "moved to the right."

It's an adaptation of this model I used to help develop an orphan's ministry at a church we used to attend. How can the Church help move orphans to the right, into loving homes?

Drawing from this speaker's concept, I want to borrow from it again and reframe it by saying that following Cooper's death, there were many people who "made it better." I believe the wide net of folks making it better for us was critically important in helping with our long-term healing trajectory.

Slow, deep breath; in through the nose, slowly, deeply, and completely, hold it briefly, and let it out slowly, deeply, and completely.

When law enforcement officers from the sheriff's office arrived at our home on the morning of October 8th to tell us our son was deceased, they made it better. From this earliest moment, our healing process—our grief—was already beginning to be moved to the right and made better.

Let me explain.

The officers who arrived were professional, compassionate, kind, and as empathetic as they could be in the most traumatic situation of our lives. The officers arrived with a chaplain who spent the morning with us as we wailed, vomited, froze, shook, and collapsed. During my years on the fire department, I responded to many suicides and interacted with law enforcement, but now I was on the receiving side of the equation.

It doesn't seem fair to me. Twenty-five years of helping complete strangers on their worst day, saving the masses one by one, and I couldn't save my son.

The officers did an exceptional job. Beyond their professionalism in sharing the tragic news of our son's death with us, they picked up Cooper's car and drove it to our house. They gave us printed material and their cell phone numbers and told us to call if we needed anything or had any questions. They did a good job of delivering very bad news, and they, all things considered, were the first people to make it better.

The crime scene investigator (CSI) later called us to ask a few questions. He was kind, professional, and eager to help the best he could. I had so many questions. I wanted to come see Cooper's body. This was not possible because all suicides in the county are investigated to ensure no foul play. This is a good thing, but it meant the chain of evidence couldn't be disrupted, and therefore, we couldn't go see Cooper. Also, many of my questions, at this time, couldn't be answered for the same reason. I asked the CSI, "Would you please go lay hands on Cooper and pray for him, and be sure to take good care of him and honor his body?" His response, "Absolutely, you have my word." I believed his conviction.

That's one thing I can say about the folks in the Midwest: in the main, on par, they are good, down-home people who do what they say they are going to do.

I have had several phone conversations with the CSI, including a very recent one, and he has been so incredibly helpful and professional. He, like the officers and chaplain, made it better.

In the first week, we also interacted with a detective from the sheriff's office. She brought over a bag of Cooper's belongings, answered my questions honestly, and was kind and compassionate toward us. She gave us hugs. She was sorry, and we knew her empathy was genuine. She, too, made it better.

I want to pause here and share my heartfelt thanks to the county sheriff's office. Further, I want to give heartfelt thanks to the law enforcement officers who do the tough work they do and let them know that, in our house, they are appreciated and respected for their noble work.

I don't want to get into politics and the cultural wars. I'm no longer interested. My son's death transcends the petulant leadership and tribalism of today's political discourse.

I want to say that on the worst day of our lives, bar none, law enforcement made it better for our family.

Said another way, our grieving and healing got off to a better start than it otherwise probably could have.

After law enforcement notified us, it was time for us to make some calls and notifications. It was brutal.

I have already written about my brother canceling his vacation and flying from Florida to our house to walk through hell with us. My brother, Jason, made it better.

I remember calling my parents. My dad answered. I asked, "Is Mom up?" "Nope, she's still sleeping." I said, "This is urgent, you need to wake her up." My dad walked in and woke Mom up, and I told them both that Cooper had taken his own life last night. I will never forget the wailing of my mom. When we talk about this now, my mom doesn't remember it; she has blacked it out of her memory.

Cooper lived near my parents while attending college at the University of Arizona (2018-2022), and he spent a lot of time with Nanny and Poppy. On weekends, breaks, and even the summer, Cooper would go to his grandparents' house and get spoiled. He would swim and golf and grill with Poppy. Swordfish on the grill was a common theme. Yeah, his death hurt them deeply.

We also had to call Cooper's brothers and tell them. CJ lives with his fiancée, Em, out of state so we felt better about telling him, as he had someone to lean on. Carse lives alone, and we did not want to tell him until somebody was there with him. Our plan to tell Carse backfired, as we called him to ask if he was with his friend, as we suspected he might be, but he was not. Carse knew something was up and demanded we tell him. So we did. It went about as well as could be expected. He was leaving the gym. He punched the inside of his car with his car keys in his hand, which broke his key fob, and he had to walk home. I stayed on the phone with him for nearly three hours, mostly in silence. Carse was literally in shock.

My parents immediately drove to pick Carse up and drive him back home with them. The next day, they all left for our house by car. Two days later, they arrived. We all hugged and sobbed in the driveway the minute they pulled in.

CJ, our oldest, and Em immediately flew into town. They did not purchase return tickets home. One way.

We drove over that morning to tell my wife's mom in person, the other Nanny. She was loving and compassionate with her daughter; it was amazing. Understand, my wife has not had the best relationship with her mom over the years, but in that moment, I witnessed a

CJ and Coop

lot of healing and a very compassionate moment between mother and daughter.

The point of sharing the above is that my parents picking Carse up so he was not alone, and then as expeditiously as possible driving to our house, my brother immediately flying out to be with us in hell, and my oldest son and his fiancée immediately flying out—they all made it better.

We circled the wagons together as a family.

Then, our friends and coworkers all made it better with food, snacks, supplies, nice text messages, phone calls, cards, art, flowers, donations, and a great show of compassion and care toward us during a very, very hard time.

They made it better.

After all the family was gathered, there was the issue of a memorial service to contend with. We wanted to do something for family only, simple, and at our house. I reached out to Fr. Michael, my friend and priest with the local Orthodox Church, and asked if he would deliver a memorial service for Cooper. Of course, he said. He and his wife, Matushka, came over and performed the service. Instantly, our house went from high stress and emotion to one of calm. Their singing was beautiful, and they brought peace with them. Every person present would corroborate this. Fr. Michael and Matushka, they made it better.

Finally, even the funeral home, and especially the funeral home manager, made it better. We had never interacted with a funeral home before, and they helped us in a very careful and compassionate manner all along the way. We wanted to see Cooper, but there were some nuances to contend with. They made it work in a beautiful way, in the chapel, and I will always be grateful we got to say "goodbye." I think this viewing was particularly meaningful to Cooper's brothers. I know it was to me.

Yes, this all sucks. I was out walking today, on what I have come to call my Trail of Tears, listening to my "Thinking of you, Cooper" playlist, and I was overcome by how real and tragic his death is. It's weird, this grief, how it comes in waves, and sometimes the waves flatten you with their weight. It's like, "Damn, this is real, I am not dreaming."

That said, our capacity to cope is building, and some sense of healing, for me, is taking place. I see the grace in that so many people and organizations made it better. I think these early "positive" experiences cast a good overall tone, helping us pivot in the right direction. I'm under no illusion—things could be different, the tone could have been set negatively from the get-go, and it would have done tremendous harm. Probably irreparable harm.

Cooper did not physically hurt anyone. We were able to view him, say goodbye, and we know where he is buried—next to his grandfather. We know we will be buried next to him one day in the future. Tragic as Cooper's death is, and it really is, I know it could have been worse. I know others actually do have it worse.

All along the way, you, dear family and friends, and others, you made it better.

My hope is that as I move forward in life, I can make it better for others, and as I have discussed, especially for young men.

With gratitude to those who made it better.

Blessed are those who make it better.

Amen.

poundmakers

When we lived in Montana for a few seasons of life, I was invited to attend a few Powwows. They spoke to me.

With Cooper's passing, I often find myself turning to art, listening to music, reading poetry—trying to find the words to express the deep place of hurt inside me.

I found a video that comes close. It's a video of Native Americans at a Powwow grieving the loss of a family member.

I imagine my wife and I, my brother, my dad, my nephew, my sons and daughter, and a few of Cooper's close friends—Ethan, Jacob, Jonathan, Chase, Nik, and Abby—sitting around this drum. We have a picture of Cooper in the center of the drum.

We breathe deep, go deep into ourselves, turn right, and then drop down again to another layer of depth in our hearts, and we sing in honor of our boy and let our tears flow.

Del otro lado, Cooper smiles. Our voices get through.

Bless the Poundmakers.[1] Thank you for giving voice to what I am having difficulty expressing.

monk or millionaire
December 14, 2023

As I continue to marinate in grief, I feel and I think. I process. In thinking, I have three major regrets as Cooper's father. I regret the day I ever put a smartphone in Cooper's hands. Secondly, though it was not my choice, I regret that I did not push back harder on Cooper's decision to major in aerospace engineering. Lastly, I regret that I was not a better listener to my son. I did not hear him. I do now.

I don't believe suicide is due to a single cause; I think it's multi-causal.

Suicide is an onion with many layers. I'm going to call it the suicide onion. I feel like I keep peeling back layer upon layer of a strong white onion, and I am standing at the cutting board crying, layer after layer. Nope, I don't wear glasses—no "not-crying-peeling-the-onion" tricks—just a full embrace of peeling the suicide onion suck fest: feeling and thinking.

Or, suicide is a long chain with many links. One broken link does not lead to suicide, nor two, or three, or maybe four. But the broken links do add up, and the more broken links there are in the suicide chain, the more the risk of suicide increases.

Broken links do not mean suicide is inevitable, but we should be mindful of rising risk.

Mt. Everest is the tallest mountain in the world. She stands tall and proud at over 29,000 feet, reaching into the heavens. She's an eternal beauty. Climbers die each year attempting to summit Everest, but more climbers die during descent—approximately 75%—than during ascent. This is interesting. I think the reason is that climbers don't leave any reserve in the tank; they give it all going up and forget they have to come back down.

Climbing deaths on Everest are not sudden, tragic events. There is a climbing system, and small events happen; links in the climbing chain get broken. A climber gets a headache, another can't feel their toes, someone is getting low on oxygen. Each event, alone, by itself, is generally manageable. But together, collectively, these events add up, and the synergy can lead to tragedy.

I don't believe Cooper suddenly took his own life. It was not random. There were many broken links in the chain—a synergy. This is how my brain is thinking about Cooper's suicide: multi-causal, an onion with many layers of complexity, broken links, synergistic.

Again, I hate writing "Cooper's suicide." I hate it. I prefer "taking his own life." A child dying is the worst day. A child dying by suicide adds so much complexity. It's a double espresso of pain and confusion. "Why?" we scream.

Back to the onion, or chain, or mountain—whichever you prefer.

In peeling back the onion, I certainly believe technology, excessive screen time, and social media have been disastrous for our youth. Cooper was a digital native; he grew up surrounded by technology in a way I did not.

We were pretty good as parents, I think, in that we limited screen time. During the week, our children were not allowed to play games—only on the weekends. During the week, Monday through Friday, it was a time to focus on school and sports, not screens.

When we ate dinner, it was at the table, together as a family, no screens. No television blaring in the background. We hold to this today. Mealtime is sacred space; we look each other in the eye and ask how the day went.

We did not give our kids smartphones until they were in 7th grade. This was our family demarcation line for a phone. If I could go back and do it again, I would not give my children smartphones until they were 25. This is hardcore, I know, and totally unrealistic. I understand.

I recently tried to do a Google search for MRI pictures of the brain, before the smartphone era and today. I cannot find good compare-and-contrast examples. I imagine technology companies and search engines would be incentivized to not show me this information.

The prefrontal cortex (PFC) in the human brain is important in impulse control—such as not taking your own life, for example. I believe technology has stunted PFC development in our youth. I believe this is one factor, a layer of the onion, in the extremely high and continually increasing suicide rates.

If I were to compare Cooper's brain and his PFC to that of a 23-year-old living in the mountains of Alaska in 1950, I don't think they'd look the same. I believe the PFC of the mountain man would be functional and operational, whereas I don't believe the PFCs of today's youth are fully developed. And this says nothing of the wiring of the rest of the brain.

We already know technology adversely impacts childhood brain development. There is increasing evidence/research for this, but I don't think we yet know how adversely technology and staring at screens almost all day is affecting brain development in our youth. My wager: it's ginormous.

Social media is also harmful to children, and I rue the day my children used social media. There is a reason most social media CEOs and executive staff don't allow their children on social media. Oddly, if you don't have a smartphone or computer, you don't have access to social media. Technology is the vehicle; social media is the hookers, pimps, and drug lords riding in the vehicle, driving to our houses, coming to play in our children's developing minds.

I believe social media does two-pronged damage to children. First, there is damage to the nervous system through hundreds of thousands of dopamine-receptor activations over the years.

Social media companies are not idiots. They have billion-dollar operating budgets and lots of time and money to research how to keep kids on the screen. Why? The short answer is profit. Your child is the market, and they have been for many years.

That little red "like" button on social media is a feedback loop. When we get likes on our posts/pictures/snaps/tweets, it activates a chemical reaction in the body, namely dopamine.

For example, an orgasm releases dopamine. So do cocaine, meth, and, to a lesser degree, the little red like button showing up on social media.

How many dopamine hits did Cooper have over his lifetime? Thousands upon thousands. Hundreds of thousands.

This level of repetition and all that nervous system activity can't be good, right? Envision many of our youth today. They have small, waxy hands that shake most of the time. These are not calloused hands. They have anxiety, are depressed, and can't talk to another person face-to-face or look them in the eye.

To put this into perspective, it took me 23 years on the fire department, dealing with a lot of stress, to develop general anxiety. Cooper was anxious at maybe 15 or 16 years old, and I know he's not alone.

His nervous system was not responding to being stalked by a lion all day, so what, then?

Humans, unless someone can prove me wrong, are evolutionary-biological creatures. I believe in God, of course, but I don't discount biological-evolutionary development either. The two are not mutually exclusive. I am both an evolutionary creature and I have a God-given eternal spirit. I have a warm spirit in my biological chest.

The second negative prong of social media is existential. Humans have a strong, overwhelming need and desire to be part of the "tribe." Why? Because one can't survive long outside the tribe, the community. It's a biological imperative to belong, and when we don't feel included in the tribe, it's harmful.

Have you ever watched an episode of the series *Alone*? If not, you should. The all-time record on *Alone* is 87 days. One cannot live very long alone, period.

Loneliness, isolation, and shame—the three-headed dragon.

The challenge with social media is there is always the perceived existential threat of being kicked out of the tribe. The threat is not real, but it is perceived as real. The brain doesn't know the difference between perceived, simulated threat and real threat. The nervous system responds accordingly.

I am arguing that one of the causes—a layer of the onion, a link in the chain—in the increased suicide rates among young people, including Cooper, is underdeveloped prefrontal cortices due to excessive screen time and technology, fried nervous systems due to repeated dopamine hits, and the perceived existential threat on social media of being kicked out of the tribe because they don't measure up.

This is why I have not been a very good Facebooker over the years, if at all. Aside from the serious privacy concerns I have, I know social media, including FB, is simply not a healthy medium in the biological-spiritual human experience.

Let's peel back another layer of the onion.

My wife is a schoolteacher and she is super savvy at science, technology, engineering, and math—STEM. One, she's just smart. But two, she had excellent math teachers growing up. Today, I believe STEM is called STEAM, as "art" has been added.

I mentioned in a previous blog post that we were, as parents, ardent Montessorians. This is true. Maria Montessori is one of my heroes, and I mean this sincerely. I've read a few of her biographies and she's a fascinating person to me. She used her training in medicine to create a solid educational methodology for, originally, orphans in the slums.

Aside from remaining tethered to objective reality, Montessori methods help pupils understand abstract concepts through concrete manipulative material, like math.

Our kids are good at math and much of their strong math skills derive, I think, from their mom and their early Montessori education. Cooper was exceptionally good at math. He had stupid math smarticles. Me, not so much.

Cooper wanted to go into aerospace engineering because the degree aligned with his math talent, but also because he believed he would ultimately make a lot of money in the field. When I pressed Cooper on why he wanted to make a lot of money, it was because he wanted to live near the ocean, and, so it seems, you need a lot of money to live near the ocean. He was not wrong. This is sad commentary on life in general, but facts are facts.

Cooper kicking a soccer ball, Windansea Beach, La Jolla, CA

However, I checked Cooper and pushed back a little. My concern with aerospace engineering was that it seemed to me that where Cooper would make his future money was necessarily in the "defense" industry. I don't think it's political to say the US weapons industry is obscene.

This is a moral, not a political, statement. If we eliminated the top five weapons manufacturers today, the world would immediately be a safer, better place. I believe this unequivocally, and I shared as much with Cooper.

Can I advocate for God and the "defense" industry? Does it help if the language is couched in "defense" or "just war" narratives?

The point is, morally, I did not want my son working in weapons proliferation to be able to live by the ocean, and sadly, this is where the money is made in aerospace engineering, in the main. As the Catholics—the Dominicans—say, the means never justify the ends. The Dominican dies hard in me.

Ultimately, I wanted to support Cooper (self-agency), and I did, but I expressed my concerns to him. I supported his degree choice, AE, and his future work.

Isn't it our job as parents to help establish moral boundaries, to be confidants rather than "best friends"? I thought it important to share the truth rather than tell Cooper what he may have wanted to hear. What I hope he heard was, "I love you, I support you no matter what, and these are my concerns..."

This tension created a friendly conversation Cooper and I would have over the last five years. We called the conversation "Monk or Millionaire." We both smiled when we had this conversation.

You see, I believe Cooper's pursuit of an aerospace engineering degree mentally broke him on some level. It's another layer of the suicide onion, a general consideration on my mind map, a possible break in one of the links on the chain. The AE degree at the University of Arizona (UA) is rigorous. I have heard it's the second or third most demanding degree program on campus, out of over 150 majors.

Over Cooper's four years, I often felt like I was running a triage unit when he would come home for breaks. He was wiped out. I know he was going hard at the frat partying and studying hard, but I would often ask him, "Is this degree worth it? Why not study economics or business administration?"

I asked him to balance his math courses with courses in the humanities. He did. He took courses in Islamic studies and Buddhism, for example.

I would even throw my old fire department logic at him: "You can't help anybody if you don't arrive safely." I would ask him, "What good is an AE degree if you're all broken down when you complete it?"

Mt. Everest—75% of fatalities occur on descent.

Cooper was not a quitter; he was tenacious in the things he started. No, tenacious is not the right word—that sounds forced. Cooper was patient and persistent in the things he started. He finished them. When Cooper was little, he would work on a 500-piece puzzle in the middle of the tiled hallway, and I would watch him come and go to the puzzle over the course of several days until it was complete.

Another good example: Cooper was a black belt in Taekwondo. He stayed the course in training over three years until he achieved his black belt rank. Slow and steady, he stayed with it.

Cooper stayed in the AE program at UA because it was an academic, intellectual challenge for his gifted mind; because he started it and wanted to complete it; and finally, because Cooper fancied having enough money so he could live near the ocean.

The thing is, Cooper knew the system—this whole thing—is rigged and is a joke. We would talk about this. I would counter, "Yes, 'the matrix' is a joke and we're all pawns. I concede."

But, I would argue, breaking bread with friends, having a bitter beer or coffee with another, hiking a mountain, skiing, petting a dog, helping another, reading a book, watching a sunrise, listening to music, gardening, praying, meditating, raising a family, loving another, laughing, and dancing—these are not nothing.

It's possible to concede the game is rigged and still live a happy life within the matrix, no?

So I would argue with Cooper, "If it's all rigged and you know it, then drop it all and become a monk. Drop out of the system. Give a full bird salute and opt out. Take your talent and walk."

I had visions of Cooper leaving America and living in one of those yellow wooden houses on the shores of some picturesque bay in Norway. He was married to a beautiful Jewish woman with long, dark curly hair, and they had two children. He fished a lot in the bay. He worked remotely for MIT or some such smart educational institution. Cooper was at peace and contented in the relative silence, and, to the degree possible, he had taken steps to remove himself from "the matrix," as he called it.

Cooper, graduation, University of Arizona, May 2022

And I used to tell him this: "You're not going to win, but resistance is important, and studies in resilience validate this. Tiny acts of resistance have meaning," I would say.

This was my "monk" vision for him, as contrasted with his millionaire vision. So we bantered about Monk or Millionaire over the years, and I am deeply grateful for these fun conversations, but also saddened that he didn't opt out, as, in retrospect, I think he would have found peace for his soul. But, as with so many things these days, we will never know.

Finally, my last major regret as Cooper's father is, I didn't listen. It's not so much that I didn't listen as that I didn't hear him.

I remember seeing this little depression meme one time. There's a little stick figure curled up in a ball in bed. Another stick figure crawls into bed with them, and they both just lie there. No words.

It's not that I was trying to problem-solve for Cooper and not listening. I listened well, I think. The problem is I did not hear him with my third ear. I did not hear what was said below the words. In hindsight, his pain is evident. My memories of past conversations are blurry, but I know now that more was said than what I heard.

If I watch a sunrise, or the moon drop over the horizon throughout a long night, or watch a dog sleeping, something is being said.

Cooper was saying something. I don't think he even knew what it was, and I never picked up on what was unsaid but said. Probably because I, too, am a product of the matrix, and I scuttle and hurry about and don't really see or hear the things moving in slower motion.

Were I a monk—and if my wife ever predeceases me, it's what I will become—I imagine, in my spiritual imagination, Cooper leaving his home in Norway to come visit me. During our visit, as he tells me about his family, the fishing, and his work, I would hear him say what he wasn't saying. I would hear him, perhaps for the first time.

If Cooper had never had a smartphone, never engaged with social media, had pursued more of the "A" in STEAM, and had I heard him with my third ear, I do believe this blog post would not have been written today.

shadow casting

As I have journeyed through this life, I have experienced hardship. I'm not alone—you've experienced hardship, too. I know that. We might call hardship suffering.

I've experienced hardship in my marriage, in my work, in my finances, in my faith, in my health, and in my relationships. As I have navigated these various hardships, it has always seemed to me there would be closure. I could see a light at the end of the tunnel. I had a sense that my stress, discomfort, and pain were temporary. Turns out, they were. I think this sense of "things are going to get better" is called hope.

As I have shared, I believe that hope is important, even more so than resilience. Even if it's rugged, we have to start somewhere.

I believe there are seasons in life. Some seasons are mountaintop highs, and some are narrow valley lows. It's hard to know how long a season will last; it could be years. Hope is difficult when we don't know how long a suffering valley will last. We pine for closure.

If you're asking me, I want the mountaintop highs all the time. I was hiking with Cooper in the mountains, and it was a good day

—a good season of life to be living in the mountains. On that day, we were, literally, on the mountaintop. Why would I not want this day, this season, every day?

But if I look back on my life, it's the lows that formed me—made me a better, stronger man. Yes, I kicked ferociously against the goads in those valleys, in the crucible, and I have rarely, with contentment, accepted when God has set me in the valley. Sadly, my childish nature is never far from me. My neck is stiff, and my heart is hard in this way. However, I am maturing, and I do better in the narrow valleys than I used to. We might call this character.

Though we all have tough seasons of life, we have good seasons, too. Perhaps if we looked deeply enough, we might even notice the rhythm of these seasons. Maybe this rhythm, this ebb and flow, is meant to help us form hope and character.

My brother has twice now had dangerous kayaking mishaps. He was stuck in the river's swift water, and there was no let-up. The water rushed by and kept rushing by—it was relentless. He almost drowned.

I had a different near-drowning experience. I was in Hawaii, on the North Shore. Body surfing seemed like an adventurous idea, until it wasn't. I, too, nearly drowned. But the waves came in rhythm and briefly let up. I had a moment to recalibrate, take a breath, and steady myself before the next wave. Rhythm.

I am suggesting there is a rhythm to the valleys and mountaintop experiences of life.

Or what is it? Six days we labor, and one day we rest. Sabbath rhythm.

Or what is it? Sacrament of reconciliation followed by sacrament of holy communion. Sacramental rhythm.

Or what is it? We fast, and then we feast. Orthodox, eucharistic rhythm.

Two weeks ago, I attended my first bereavement/support group for those who have lost a child. It's hosted through a local The Compassionate Friends group. The group is small, and I think that's a good thing. It's good if few have lost children, but it's not good if parents are grieving alone.

The loss of a child is not a path you want to walk alone. In fact, I don't think it's possible to walk this path alone.

Our group, on this particular night, was small: three of us— myself and two mothers who have lost children.

We lit candles for our children, shared stories about them, and shared in our grief and our hopes. We had smiles and tears. It was very good for me to know I am not alone in the complexity of my feelings, in my pain, and also in my hope. This was the first time I have met with others who have lost a child, sat and talked to them, heart to heart. This was not trivial space; this is the place where we go to collect coins in the deep places, together.

I mentioned in a previous post that this is a tough gang to get beat into. And it is. What is surprising to me, what scares me, is that losing a child is not one of those hardships you get over. I don't see closure or light at the end of the tunnel for this suffering. I am having difficulty discerning a rhythm.

I know I/we have been permanently impacted mentally, emotionally, physically, spiritually, and socially. Forever.

It's not that I don't have hope for a better future—I do—but there's something. I know in my deep place that things are never going to be the same and that something very, very profound has happened. I can't shake the largeness of this.

And by the way, God, if you're reading, and I think you are, I still think you got it wrong.

I walk with a shadow now—it's always there. Sometimes, my shadow is wide, long, and it can't be missed; it's twice the length of my body. At other times, it's high noon, the sun is right above me, and I only see a tiny slice of my shadow. It's barely there, but damn, it's still there.

As a bereaved father, I am now a shadow caster. I walk around casting my shadow about, and most of the world does not notice. They're not shadow noticers; they don't know. My wife knows. The mothers know.

Shadow casting is paradoxical. On one side of the shadow casting coin, I want the world to know my son, Cooper, died. I want to scream in the world's face, "Do you freaking know what's happened?!" And on the other side of the shadow casting coin, I don't want people to know. I want to hide my shadow, get in and get out, and get back to my cave to drink herbal tea with yak's milk.

I'm a paradoxical shadow caster.

As I sat with my new friends, fellow shadow casters, in my child loss bereavement/support group, they both wept and were weary in their bones with grief and sorrow. How they longed for their children. No words necessary; I understood. Sacred space. A pocket full of coins.

I am touched by my new friends. I love them both, and I knew, in spending time with them, it's not going to be okay, but it's going to be okay.

I shared with my wife after the meeting, "I don't think this— this empty void of pain, Melancholy Man—is going away." She looked at me like, "Yeah, I know." She already knew, of course. As usual, two steps ahead of me.

So what then?

I discuss with my wife that we must heal in some aspect, otherwise, what? For example, we are better today than on ground zero day. What's happened then? I call it healing.

She disagrees. She says she's never going to heal. But I wonder about this language, and I have questions. What my wife is saying, I think, is something along the lines of Robin Williams to Matt Damon in *Good Will Hunting*: "If you or anyone else ever even comes close to intimating that I will forget my son and my love for him, 'I will end you. I will f***ing end you. Got that, Chief?'"

As a bereaved father, I get stuck in this place. How do I love and honor my son and heal without forgetting him?

So we reframe the conversation. I read about this in *Bearing the Unbearable*. Instead of discussing that our hurt and pain will go away—they probably won't—we rather consider that our ability to cope rises to run parallel with the pain.

As parents, we don't stop hurting, as it were. Rather, we get stronger, our resilience builds, steeling takes place. Maybe we find hope. I hope we find hope. Mostly, more than anything, I want Cooper's siblings to have hope for their futures. There is so much to look forward to.

There will be suffering, sure, and there will be seasons spent in the narrow valleys, but this is not bad. This is life. Formation is taking place; hope and character are being formed.

I see this with my wife and my new friends, the mothers. Their hurt, pain, and grief—their longing for their child—is right there, barely underneath the surface, accessible in an instant. But also, they are strong and courageous.

I get out of bed every day and navigate life, and this feels like victory to me. Am I getting 1% better each day? Yes and no. It's two steps forward and one step back. Am I winning the day? Most days, yes.

I'm a paradoxical shadow caster now, searching for a new rhythm in my life. I know my shadow is not leaving me, but I want to learn to dance with it, long shadow or tiny slice shadow. I am learning to stand together with my shadow, do spiritual edgework with it, form rugged hope with it.

I got beat into this gang, and they gave me a shadow. They told me to find my rhythm, and maybe some hope.

Miss you, Boy.

Dad

~

aftermath

I underestimated the emotional impact of the Christmas holiday. I thought, "It's a special day, sure, but still, it's just another day without my son. Why would it be different from all the other days?"

I wish I could explain why it was different, but I can't. It's felt, sensed. It was heavier without Cooper here, with a constant void, an emptiness. Melancholy Man set up camp and stayed a few weeks.

Taking down the Christmas tree ornaments saddened me. So many little ornaments made by my guy when he was just a small fry.

Four stockings hung by the fireplace with care.

Chinese food on Christmas Eve—no Cooper.

Christmas Eve drinks and board games—no Cooper here to laugh with.

It's amazing how we build routines and annual habits into our lives, and these threads give shape to our days, anchor us, tie us together.

Not gonna lie, the holiday season set me back a bit. It was harder than I anticipated. I underestimated it. One step backward, for sure.

First Christmas and New Year without Cooper, in the books. Very sad, heartbreaking, difficult, and emotional.

And yet, some new patterns and threads were woven.

I went out and played pool and drank beer with Carse. One evening, after about five games of pool, I said, "I need a break for a bit." As we sat at our table, I asked Carse, "How are you doing? How are you processing your brother's death?"

In his own way, Carse opened up to me and shared his emotions, his thoughts. That moment alone was worth our time together.

Cooper and Carse

Playing pool and having a few beers with my son was enjoyable; it was fun. It took my mind off things, gave my brain a break. I was able to smile and relax, let my shoulders down, just be for a little bit.

I also drove out to the cemetery with CJ and spent some time near Cooper's gravesite. We talked a bit, prayed, took it all in.

What is it exactly one is supposed to do at a gravesite? I don't know, but I always feel better after I visit. I say things, I pray, I show up. The presence feels honoring. It feels warm to be there. But it's hard, too.

The drive out to the cemetery gave me time with CJ to ask how he is doing, how he is processing. We both agreed that we have had anger show up in our grieving. We love Cooper, and we have also been angry at him for doing this. He hurt a lot of people, deeply and forever.

CJ and Cooper

But we both admit that our anger is fleeting. We love Cooper and realize he was hurting, and it wasn't really Cooper who took his life.

I imagine it this way: Cooper was carrying a tremendous amount of pain. When he took his own life, he dispersed that pain to his family and friends. The pain I have in his absence is only a fraction of the pain he was carrying, as other family and friends have their share. So if I know how badly I hurt, and I am only carrying one share of pain, a fraction, then wow, I don't know how Cooper did it for so long.

Yeah, these firsts are tough. First Christmas without Cooper, first New Year's Day. There will be more, and I can't say that I really look forward to them.

I am doing better than ground zero day for sure. I can feel myself getting stronger and gaining balance and equilibrium. I still hurt, of course, and I walk around daily with an aching emptiness in my soul, my shadow casting about, but I do feel stronger and more healed than before.

I am not healed, but some healing has taken place.

My wife and I still talk, we still process, and we still run into the same unanswerable questions. But we talk it out nonetheless.

Cooper's death is not like the death of my father or my grandparents. I worked through the grieving process following their deaths, and I feel fine today. I miss them, surely, but I remember them with love and fondness. Very few regrets. This is where the "stages of grief" make sense to me. With their deaths, I believe I am on the backside of the grieving process. I worked through something, and I am at peace with their deaths.

Not so with Cooper. It seems to me it will be like a pinball arcade game, the ball bouncing around side to side through these stages of grief. Bing, bing, bing. The ball falls through the grief levers and gets shot back up into the stages to bounce around all over the place.

But there are moments. I do savor them.

Out of the blue, I received a very nice text message from a former student yesterday. He's a full-time firefighter now, got married a year ago, and they have a newborn son. He sent me a picture and told me he missed me. In a good way, it broke me up. I found myself in tears, standing in my kitchen. Grown-ass man with tears running down my cheeks, jingling the coins in my pocket.

He didn't know about Cooper, and I didn't tell him. I didn't want to spoil the vibe.

It's not lost on me, and it's painful. I know my son won't know the deep, warm, long glow of marriage and the beautiful joy of being a father. This is heartbreaking, and I can't change it.

The text exchange with my beloved former student gave me hope because it helped me to focus on my future, and it clarified some things for me. The thing is, I know how my body feels and reacts when the Holy Spirit is speaking to me, and in this text exchange, the Spirit was with me, giving me direction.

It was good to know God has not left me. I never thought He did, really, but He has been silent.

In this new year, God willing, I hope to move back into education, into the classroom. It's what I am passionate about, something I am decent at—teaching. I imagine teaching young students and giving them my very best. This is aligned with my strengths and passion, and most importantly, it feels honoring to Cooper. Cooper would be proud of the message I received from my student.

Here I am, Lord. Full send me.

as if

January 22, 2024

My heart longs for my son, Cooper. Every single day. As if.

It's winter. My bones ache from this relentless cold; I am chilled from the inside out. The sky is a sorrowful gray, sad and droopy. These winter clouds press down into the treetops, seeking life and color. Any color, even the bare, brown, leafless trees of winter. Then there are the gold-leafed trees, refusing to give up their color. The gold leaves hang lifeless, yet I honor their tenacity.

It's as if this gray, drab winter mirrors the winter clouds in my soul. I look out the window, then search inside. Same. My heart is consubstantial with the clouds.

I've read that parents who have lost a child can develop a "new" relationship with their deceased child. When I first read this, it struck me as quackery.

On further reflection, and as time slowly marches on, the time marches on, I have reconsidered. I think I understand.

I carry Cooper in my heart and in my mind. I walk with him—in my spirit, in my will, in my soul. He's not gone; he lives within me. All of my children live in me. My wife, too. And my parents. Lest I forget my dogs, them too.

I converse with Cooper, bounce my emerging ideas off him, ask for his input on my upcoming decisions, and pause more frequently to sense his spirit. Are you there, Boy? What have you got to say? And oh, by the way, you've got some explaining to do...

In this way, it's as if I do have a new relationship with Cooper, despite the winter clouds searching the brown leafless treetops in my heart. I have tenacious golden leaves, too. A gift, a grace.

Lest you worry, does Cooper answer me? Not so much as I can tell. Do I sense his spirit when I pause? No, not really, not in the main.

But strange things happen. It's as if there's a little more magic, mystery, and miracle within my grasp. Or perhaps I'm just more open to being surprised by magic, mystery, and miracle in my life.

And why not?

I keep my routine. Each day, I touch Cooper's leather wallet and his stainless steel necklace, after opening the door to let his soul in and out, and I tell him I love him. Then a tingling runs up my back. It's a strange thing.

The wind chime, chimes, when I whisper morning prayers, and this is mysterious. How is it the Holy Spirit moves again? I have questions.

Not within my grasp, but I see a single red cardinal sitting on the backyard fence in zero-degree weather against a backdrop of snow. It sits, still, fluffed up and aware. This presents as magic.

Why, on this day, is a cardinal sitting there, alone? What message is being sent?

Wind chime to cardinal, cloud cover to treetop—in nature and in the soul, the great spirit of life runs back and forth.

In this season of life, do I want to listen to the magical stories of gypsies as they weave great tales of the dead, or do I want to dive further into Western rationalism and understand my stages of grief?

As if.

~

good grief

Chapter 1

I don't know why, but I've always imagined my life unfolding in three narrative arcs—three overlapping yet distinct phases. If my life's a story, there are three chapters.

Inshallah.

My first chapter was physical, the second intellectual, and the third, I intend, will be spiritual.

In my estimation, the first phase of my life is complete. I worked a fire department career, and I chalk this up to the physical phase.

Don't get me wrong, firefighters are incredibly smart people. Matthew B. Crawford, author of *Shop Class as Soul Craft*,[1] argues for the intelligence of those who work in the trades.

It's why Maria Montessori's method is brilliant. If all knowledge is derived through the senses—and I believe it is—then it stands to reason that those who work with their hands, interacting with objective reality, are intelligent.

Meaning to say, firefighters, plumbers, electricians, and so on are intelligent people because they learn about the world through their senses.

Also, firefighting is spiritual work. When I broke bread with my brothers at the kitchen table for lunch, dinner, and morning coffee each and every shift, I was partaking in something like a Eucharist.

Nevertheless, firefighting is physically demanding, and I consider the chapter of my life lived in the physical arc as complete.

Chapter 2

After I retired from the fire service, I transitioned to work in higher education—teaching. I think of teaching as aligned with the intellect, though I'm not dismissing the spiritual and relational aspects of it. Certainly, there is a spiritual component to teaching, at least when it's done well.

These imagined chapters of my life do have overlap. I'm sharing a construct, a heuristic that has given my life shape, a trajectory to follow.

Incidentally, I think this lack of shape and trajectory is part of what's hurting young men, causing them to despair. So many young men lack a sense of purpose and cohesion in their lives. Knowing your "why" is important. Or knowing the general outline of your arc(s) is important.

In the months before Cooper's death (BCD), I felt my intellect was on fire. My brain seemed to be working well. I was taking a class through the University of Helsinki to learn the Finnish language, enrolled in a Christian master's degree program, and gearing up to take a weeklong course at the Massachusetts Institute of Technology.

And then, bam!

I am thankful I read *Shattered: Surviving the Loss of a Child*[2] in the early days after Cooper's death (ACD). It helped me understand that my life had forever changed and that there would be mental and intellectual impacts.

Indeed, there have been.

While I've recovered some of my intellectual functioning, I am not where I left off. Maybe I never will be, and that's okay. My brother says it will probably take a year or two. I think he's right.

My wife and I recently watched the Netflix movie, *Good Grief*. It was the trailer that lured me in. In the first twenty seconds of the trailer, the main character, Marc (played by Dan Levy), says:

> "I've been reading that the brain is like a muscle. It's why getting over a death is so hard. Because your brain has been trained to feel things for a person, when they go away your head is still operating under the impression that it should feel those things for that person, like muscle memory." — *Good Grief*, Trailer

When I saw this trailer, I had to watch the movie. This 20-second soundbite resonated deeply with me. Yes, this makes sense to me. My brain is still operating, in some sense, as if Cooper is here, but he's not. My brain is lagging behind reality; it's been "trained" to love him, think of him, feel for him, call him, text him, converse with him, etc.

How long does it take to unwind 23 years of unconditional conditioning?

Another thing, I recently read an article on grief that popped up in my Facebook feed. It's written by Marie Peltonen, discussing research on grief by Astrid Swan at the University of Helsinki.

Marie writes:

> "In the past few decades, research on grief in the fields of psychology and neuroscience has produced fresh insights on the topic. For example, functional magnetic resonance imaging (fMRI) has demonstrated that the same brain regions are activated when grieving as when navigating to a destination.
>
> In concrete terms, grief can thus be described as the presumed route to a loved one ceasing to exist. At the same time, coping with grief has become medicalized, and the focus on overcoming grief may result in harmful expectations." —Marie Peltonen, University of Helsinki[3]

I've read three books on grief following Cooper's death, and these few sentences alone make more sense to me than all the material in the books.

I am trying to navigate to a destination: Cooper. My son is "lost" (or I am lost), and I am trying to find a route to him, but he no longer exists in this world. While I know Cooper is not here, my brain, out of muscle memory, is still operating as if.

This, I think, is grief—trying to navigate to a destination (a loved one) out of mental habit, training, and years of conditioning, to a destination (a loved one) that is no longer there.

Notwithstanding the routing problems, I simply miss my boy.

Finally, the last part of that quote is worth reflecting upon: "Coping with grief has become medicalized, and the focus on overcoming grief may result in harmful expectations."

There's a reason mountaintop villages have shamans. There's a reason people hole up and drink yak's milk with the Nepalese.

I'm stuck in chapter 2. Or maybe chapter 2 has a poor ending, and it's on to chapter 3 sooner than I anticipated...

Chapter 3

?

∽

cracked ones

A few weeks back, on impulse, I asked my wife, "Do you care if I drive to Tennessee to see my brother and stay for the weekend?" She didn't mind, so I asked my brother the same. He said, "Get on out here."

I drove to Tennessee, just east of Knoxville—about a 12-hour drive from my house. Part of what I was looking for on this trip was, in fact, those 12 hours of drive time by myself, to think, reflect, and zone out. I was able to think about Cooper, grief, this pain, this process, our family, the future, hope, my faith, and all the things.

My time in Tennessee with my brother was good too, because I was able to put my physical body and mind in a new space for a weekend. All the reminders of Cooper I have at home—which are not bad—I was able to take a break from. I was able to breathe a little more deeply for three days, and this deeper breathing has stayed with me since I got back home.

We stayed busy in Tennessee. We did a pub crawl in downtown Knoxville, drank some brilliant craft beers, smoked a fine cigar, and ate an iconic meal. The sun was out, the weather was exceptionally beautiful, and it was very nice to be with my brother. I also spent time with loved ones and family.

We're four months in, post-Cooper's death, and I guess I would say to those going through grief: if your mind and heart have been pining for a road trip, take it. Go. I don't think you will be disappointed.

That said, it was nice to be back home with my wife and daughter. I have found through this experience that it's very hard for me to be away from my wife (and daughter) and our home for very long. My home has become my cave in Nepal, where I drink my yak milk.

An Observation.

My emotions are all mixed up in the months following Cooper's death, in my grief. As an example, my wife and I recently watched a romantic comedy on Netflix. Great show, good clean fun, happy and emotional. But there were emotions. It's quite strange that even my good and happy emotions are now showing up mixed with grief.

My wife is experiencing the same thing at school, where she teaches second graders. She will have some good emotions that have nothing to do with Cooper and grief, but they still express themselves as related to Cooper and grief.

I want to say, as I am experiencing grief, my emotions are a mixed bag. Even good, happy, fun emotions that have nothing to do with grief show up as tinged and colored with grief.

Another Thing.

My previous boss at the university, a fine woman and friend, texted me recently and asked if I wanted two tickets to the college basketball game. Of course! I took my daughter, Little Miss Sunshine, to the game, and she loved it.

I had a good time too, but I did learn that it was too much stimulation. I am learning in my grief that I can enter environments that are overstimulating in a way that wouldn't have bothered me before Cooper's death.

Incidentally, we were at our monthly *The Compassionate Friends* meeting last night, and one of the mothers said that her life has been lived in two epochs, so to speak. There is her life before her son died, and her life after his death. There is indeed a demarcation line for those who have experienced significant loss. Before Cooper's death (BCD), a basketball game would not have registered for me. After Cooper's death (ACD), I'm not sure I'm inclined to attend future sporting events, or events where there is too much going on. A new reality.

Ending.

In the post I wrote, *Aftermath*, I spoke about how hard Christmas was. It surprised me and set me back a few steps in my grief. I've had another event like that recently. We have been patiently waiting to receive Cooper's death certificate from the state's coroner's office. A few weeks back, before my trip to Tennessee, we received it.

Along with the death certificate, I had asked the coroner's office for the autopsy and toxicology reports. There was something about actually getting these reports and reading them that set me back a few steps in my grief. It was really hard reading, "Manner of death: suicide."

Also, the autopsy report went through some of the basic mechanics of death—not in detail, but a little more than I knew —and while I already knew it, it was still simply hard to read.

Cooper's toxicology report was a nothing burger. He had a few beers on board, below the legal limit, which we already knew, and that's it. In a very weird way, this was kind of disappointing.

There was a part of me secretly hoping for him to be loaded with drugs, to help me rationalize and explain his death. "Ahhh," I would say, "he was sky-high and not in his right mind; now this makes more sense."

Truth Be Told.

Cooper was not in his right mind. He was suffering from a mental health crisis.

The 55-year-old sedentary accountant died from a heart attack, after stressing for the last 20 years over his finances.

The 50-year-old woman died of ovarian cancer.

The 88-year-old grandfather died of Parkinson's disease.

Tragic as these examples are, they don't cause us to revolt to the level of stigmatization. We sort of accept them on some level as tragedies of life. We don't like them, nor should we, but we have familiarity with these stories. They flow with the fabric of life.

The 23-year-old recent college grad died of mental health disease, via self-harm.

We revolt. And we should. And I want to frame Cooper's death in light of a disease process, not unlike cardiovascular disease, cancer, and Parkinson's. A disease process which also has crisis inflection points—exacerbations.

We should not normalize suicide; it's not okay. But we should not stigmatize it either. Let's talk about it.

What's been amazing to me in these last four months, as I have written this blog, is the number of people who have opened up and shared with me their own stories of mental health issues and suicidal ideations. As I have exposed myself, opened up, and been vulnerable in my writing, people feel trust in sharing with me.

To all those who have a semi-colon[1], blessings and love upon you.

To those not feeling it, you are loved and cherished, and you really are enough, just exactly as you are. Feel the ground, take a deep breath, slowly, deeply, and completely.

It's the cracked ones who let the light in. And your journey is exquisite.

9-8-8 if you need it. No shame.

resilience

February 23, 2024

I have been a teacher of resilience. For real. I'll spare you the details and save them for another time.

There's a particular movie I like to share and talk about in my resilience classes: *Leave No Trace*.[1]

Leave No Trace is the story of a combat veteran suffering from mental health issues while raising his daughter in the forest on the outskirts of Portland, Oregon.

The father and daughter are, generally speaking, doing well. They are happy. They are together. They are laughing. But the state has a different view. A man can't be raising his daughter in the woods; this is not normal behavior. Father and daughter get arrested, and they are pipelined into the system, where the state government and non-profits try to "help" them.

The reason I like this movie as a discussion piece for resilience is that it brings up three important questions that demand reflection and consideration. First, who judges what "doing well" after adversity looks like? Secondly, who judges what "adversity" is? And finally, is resilience an internal feeling or observed external behaviors and competencies, or both? The point is, there are judgments made in resilience. Who's making them?

As I've been writing about child loss, I've been using the metaphor of holing up in a Nepalese cave, drinking yak's milk with the shamans to heal.

I'm not literally holed up with the shamans in Nepal, but I ask you, if I were, would I be wrong?

Cooper died. If I bought a plane ticket tomorrow to Nepal and left for three months, and this brought great solace to my soul and helped me heal, would this be a resilient move?

In another scenario, if those who have lost a child show up to work and do their jobs well, even though there's a gaping hole of sadness and empty loss in their chest that nobody can see, and they weep all day long on the inside, but nobody knows, and they smile on the outside—is this resilience?

They (we) look resilient, but what's going on inside, and does this matter in resilience?

Let's say, for the sake of clarity, that resilience is both an internal state of wellness and external competencies that can be observed by others. I both feel good in my chest, subjectively, and I behave like a competent adult in the domains of my life— people see me doing well (at work, for example).

Resilience: after the loss of my son, I care for myself, my family, and I do all the things at home and at work, and I smile—and my smile is a genuine reflection of my insides.

All good. Question: how long should it take to arrive at this place? How long will family and friends, society, give me to find warmth in my chest, strength in my bones, a smile on my face, and the ability to do all the things at home and at work?

In all manner of Western society, our culture strives for efficiency. More, better, faster. Is there a bypass in this system for the loss of a child? Doubtful.

I've only been in the bereaved parent game for four months, and my observation is this: those who have lost a child are rushed along to heal. As a result, many parents (grandparents, siblings, and friends) smile and fake it. Meanwhile, parents and siblings cry rivers of tears on the inside—and nobody knows.

Ought they to know? Excuse me, Jackwagon, could you pull your head out of your self-absorbed backside for two seconds and acknowledge my pain?

As for myself, when Cooper died, I resigned from my job immediately. It's a little more nuanced than this, but let's not let details ruin a good story, shall we?

For the last four months, I've been holed up in my home (my Nepalese cave) drinking yak's milk (coffee, tea, water, craft beer) and hanging with the shamans (prayer, spiritual reading, and attending church here and there).

I wanted to marinate in my grief and take it on the chin. Give it to me. If I can't take it, I accept death. Only bury me standing— as an act of defiance.

It's not been easy. I am grateful I've had this time to find some healing, to slowly think through everything and to process at the level of my soul.

God is the breath within the breath. At this level, I wanted to stand alone before God and have a serious conversation, out back, just the two of us. I'm serious. If You're going to lay this one on me, Lord, You better be ready to dance. I want to press my nose up against Your nose and look into Your eyes.

I digress. Through this time and deeper introspection, I have found some healing. I do have a sense of warmth and radiance in my chest again, though it comes and goes. But it's staying longer. A smile, too.

Yes, I get things done, too.

Over these last four months, I have grocery shopped, cooked, and cleaned. Not a big deal to a retired firefighter, this is what we did. My wife is working full-time, and I have striven to take the load off her so she can heal. My wife is approaching her grief in drips. It's healing for her to be at work, to turn her mind off in relation to Cooper, and then come home and process a little at a time.

She's sipping wine, I'm doing shots of tequila.

But notice: whereas I have been exploring the dark wilderness in my heart, drinking yak's milk with the shamans and praying, my wife has been working and crying on the inside.

Both resilient moves, but it looks different.

I start work next week, part-time. I'm back at it, and I feel really good about it. My cave has done me well.

I still have grief, sadness, a great sense of loss, and I imagine I always will. I don't see this going away. But I do see the rough edges smoothing out. The intensity is gone, except for a few brief moments here and there.

In the end, this all still seems incredibly tragic to me. I still feel, with every bone in my body, that the Universe got it wrong. I believe that. This was not meant to be. It's a glitch. But I'm no dummy; I am certain every parent who has lost a child feels this. But it is a glitch, right, to have a child predecease you?

Mostly, I miss my son, Cooper. He was a good boy to be sharing life with. He made this world a better place with his presence. He certainly made me happy as a father. I was blessed to have him for 23 years.

One last thought for today. For the better part of the last four months, I have spent a lot of time looking at pictures of Cooper. I still do, but I am now very intentional about looking at the pictures of my three other children, Cooper's brothers and sister, and thinking, reflecting, and praying over them.

I'm trying to say, I'm playing peekaboo with the future—with hope—and I think this is a good thing.[*]

---

[*] Appendix B: Practical Resilience

nearing six months

Hello, Friends.

March is flying by, and we will soon find ourselves resting squarely on April 8th. It's hard to believe that nearly six months have passed since October 8th, the day Cooper put on his angel wings and halo and left us. Man, that was a rough day. They don't get tougher.

As you know, I've been writing through my grief. When Cooper first died by self-harm, I knew immediately that I didn't want to sweep his death under the rug. Too many families do this, particularly with suicide. Everyone is left to guess and wonder what happened to the 23-year-old boy. I didn't want that.

It seems there is a sense of shame for parents when a child dies by suicide. I feel it, I sense it. I am not immune to these feelings.

To be fair, to each their own. I have no qualms with how people choose to handle death in their family, it's personal and a family decision.

I knew, for me (us), we were going to set the lamp on the lamp-stand and shine bright through the darkness. We simply have to start talking about young men and suicide. It is a massive problem.

Almost immediately after Cooper's death, I wrote a letter to family and friends and sent it out via text and email. The responses surprised me. Family and friends said, "You need to share this with others." That was the beginning of my blog. The first two posts were originally private letters to family and friends.

The most popular blog post is *Crippin*, written on November 28th, 2023.

What's been most uplifting throughout my grief writing has been the wonderful words of encouragement I've received from family, friends, and friendly folks just dropping a note of grace. Grace word bombs, instead of micro-atomic bombs.

Below is a sample of the words that have lifted me over the last six months. To those who wrote them, thank you. Deep bow. I accept your grace, and I love you for it.

> *"Thank you, Kelly, for your wonderful, insightful thoughts these past few months."*

> *"I've been reading Kelly's blog posts and can't stop thinking about what he writes. I feel that in his pursuit to heal and find meaning as to why Cooper took his life, Kelly is going to help many people find meaning and hope in their own lives."*

> *"Thank you so much for sending this. Grief is such a roller coaster, and he talks about it so incredibly."*

> *"Kelly, your words have opened my eyes to so many things about life and grief. My current grief is nothing compared to the loss of a*

child, but your blog has helped me so much! You and your family are so incredibly special, and the strength you have is awesome. I am definitely not good at expressing myself with words, but your words truly inspire me to try in a personal diary. Thank you!"

"Those are amazing words written with so much emotion and love! I cried through almost all of his message and could truly feel his pain!"

"I have been really enjoying your blog posts—CJ mentioned to me today that reading them provides comfort, and I agree. It is helpful in my healing process to hear your perspective, thoughts, wonderings, and stories. I mentioned this to CJ today, but I think your talent with writing is not something one can learn; it's something you're born with."

"Your blog was beautiful! It made me really stop and think about what's really important in life. Thanks for sharing this, and I'm so sorry for your loss."

"Kelly, I've always enjoyed reading your past blogs—you're such a talented writer. This one speaks to my heart. I pray that the writing process helps with the grief in some way. The way you explained what it's like to have a child missing was surreal, and the sculptures took my breath away. Thanks for sharing. Looking forward to future posts."

"These blogs are honestly the most amazing things I've ever read. It is so YOU, Kelly, that while you are trying to make sense of your tragic loss, you are also helping others."

"Reading these blogs is explaining exactly what we have gone through and done ourselves over the last 11 months. We are coming up on the one-year mark, and more questions keep coming up. I'll PM you more as I don't want to write a novel on your post. No, I don't know what it's like to lose my child, but I know the pain of what it's like to lose someone who took their own life. You

and I think so much alike, and here I thought I was the only one whose mind worked the way it does, trying to make sense of this tragic event. I'm always here to talk, bounce ideas off of. My husband swears I should have been a detective in my life."

"I recently lost my niece, so your blogs are putting words to our grieving as well…"

"Kelly, thank you for sharing your writing! I can only imagine the amount of weeping that has happened and will continue as you grieve!"

"Kelly, your blogs are so powerful to me."

"Oh man, what a beautiful blog. Just finished reading this, and I am in tears, man. What a beautiful, strong family you have, and so amazing how they all pulled together. I hug my son a little tighter and tell him I love him more often since I started reading your blogs. I can't even imagine the pain. Thank you for sharing all of this. You're a great writer. Godspeed."

"Beautifully written! I love your vulnerability—thank you for sharing. My thoughts and prayers are with you and your family."

"Such an awesome read, Kelly. Incredible. Thinking of you and your family."

"You describe this shadow-casting, coin-collecting gang with such clarity. This particular post hit hard."

"Every time I read your blogs, my heart breaks for you. Your descriptions lead us to love our own children deeper and savor the time with them. Still praying for you!"

"I loved your blog. I've been melancholy the last two days. All the kids I lost to addiction, they were like my children. I can relate to your grief. They all killed themselves. I talk to a kid I took care of eight years ago. He was lonely, with mixed feelings about wanting

to live. I've had to be resilient for others. Thank you for sharing your journey."

"Great insights, Kelly. You help others with these posts! One thing I fight with is tremendous guilt. I have since learned that a sudden death typically results in a greater level of guilt and shame—heart-wrenching emotions for sure. Like you, I am slowly but surely remembering the good and trying to be thankful for the ten years we had. Love to you and yours."

"Thank you all for your love and understanding. I do not feel that anyone else understands completely, and feeling like a burden to them—too heavy to bear the pain of seeing me or hearing me in so much pain and not being able to help—but just simply having people who unfortunately understand this depth of sadness, loss, and grief makes me feel a little less alone. I feel so very alone in this a lot. But you guys help me a lot, and I agree, Kelly's blog is very well written and expresses feelings into words I wish I knew how to do."

"I just want to say I read Kelly's blog, and he has such a gift with words. He puts exactly into words things I've felt for years that I can't explain or get out. Thank you, Kelly. It has been healing for me, the sharing of your blog. Hugs to you and Victoria. I know we are all on this journey of grief, but the important thing to remember is that we are not alone. We have each other."

"They say words are not enough, yet your words will help you and others go through the journey of handling such a tremendous loss. I love you and will always keep Cooper and his smile in my heart. 'Un abrazo, mi hijito.'"

"I have four grown-up kids, and I cannot fathom what you're going through, but your writings are inspiring!"

"Your journey is so familiar, and your words so vivid and real. Thank you for sharing pieces of Cooper with us."

"Stumbled onto your blog. Your grief is deeply felt in your eloquent blog. My husband and I are eight and a half years out from our son's death. Being able to share your thoughts is powerful. Keep talking and sharing your journey, with your wife, your children, others who you trust with your words. We hear you, we share your brokenness."

"I have been so touched by your beautiful words about your unimaginable pain. Your blog has been so touching; reading through tears, I feel so blessed to hear your story."

"Thank you for this inspiring read that reminds us to search for the little nuggets of gratitude that can be found in even the most tragic situations."

"You are making it better by sharing your deeply heartfelt story with us. Thank you!"

"Just incredible… I can visually and soulfully feel it. I just ache for all involved in similar pain."

"Keep writing; it's not only good for your soul but for your readers' souls, as well."

"Kelly, your writing touches the soul of the reader."

"Kelly, you are such an inspiration, a talented writer. I'm enjoying your journals, which you should turn into self-care essays that can help others. You've gotta know Cooper's right with you while you're putting—as we used to say back in the day—'pen to paper.'"

"Thank you so much. Thank God there aren't many people who know this kind of pain. But it's also good to know that we aren't alone in our grief… Thank you for your blog. It resonates with my husband and me so much. It's been 44 days since my son took his life. We've never prayed so hard in our lives as we have these last 44 days… Your blog is so insightful. Once again, thank you…

Again, THANK YOU for this blog. It's not easy sharing this with the world, but my husband (who's been reading it as well) and I are grateful to you for doing so... Thank you again for expressing what those of us behind you on this path are feeling."

I look forward to writing a new blog post soon. I have started a new part-time job, and surprisingly, it's been challenging for me to find the time to sit down and get into the flow of writing.

Blessings.

toll for thee
March 30, 2024

Here I am again, at the public library. I have my usual seat, looking out the window. I come here to write, hoping to minimize distractions and, perhaps, enter a sacred space. Unlike my last writing visit, there's no snow today. Spring is visibly here, and color is pressing into the landscape. Trees are budding with yellow and purple flowers, and the grass in the park is sprinkled with yellow dandelions. Children are playing on the playground across the street. I see a hive of activity. I'm not worried about the children; the ground is padded with a green recycled petroleum composite, and parents are anxiously hovering within arm's reach.

A homeless man is resting comfortably in a chair ten feet from me, taking a nap, seeking refuge. Maybe he lost a son and could never put it back together. I'd understand.

In early Spring 2023, I took a graduate course in Spiritual Formation. We studied Dallas Willard, a renowned theologian and philosopher. Willard's work has stayed with me over the last few months, and I spend a lot of time contemplating his ideas, especially now.

Willard suggests that the human person is made up of several overlapping layers. At our core, we have a spirit, sometimes called the heart or will. We have a mind with thoughts and feelings, a physical body, a social nature, and, ultimately, an outward-facing soul that interacts with the world and ties the spirit, mind, body, and social aspects of our life together.

I'm simplifying here, but the idea is that there is a lot going on within a human being that animates our life. Willard argues that as we bring these various components (layers) of ourselves into alignment with God, we begin to behave and look more like Godly creatures.

Christ-likeness, as it were, is about aligning the various layers of ourselves with the Divine.

This framework has helped me process my grief.

A few weeks ago, I had a long conversation with my second child, my son. We were discussing how much Cooper's death has impacted our ability to think, remember, and cognitively function—especially in the early weeks and months after his passing. He shared with me that when he tells people about Cooper, he shares the story in fragments. This fragmentation isn't purposeful; it's just how his narrative comes out, how he's processing. That sounds about right to me. It's a fragmented story because it's so challenging to make sense of—tragic, unexpected, final.

My wife had a great spring break in March. She met with beloved friends for hours and was able to talk about and process Cooper's death with another mother who lost a son seven years ago under similar circumstances. But also, during this Spring break, my wife was able to see the doctor about some physical ailments she's been experiencing, none of which were present before Cooper died.

My social life today is not what it was before Cooper passed. I don't have a desire to spend much time with people or in social settings for too long. I find I need whole days alone to process, grieve, walk, listen to sappy songs, cry, write, pray, think, reflect, and wonder about it all.

I'm experiencing the loss of Cooper as total, consistent with a holistic view of the human person as described by Willard. All my parts and layers are impacted—my spirit aches, my mind is foggy, my emotions are tangled in complexity, my body has pains it never had before, my social life is stunted, and my soul, the part of me that ties it all together and interfaces with the world around me, is numb, smudged, little, dry, thirsty, nauseous, and porous.

These emotions. Emotional intelligence, emotional literacy, emotional complexity.

Around 2006 or so, I visited a counselor for six sessions because I was stressed at work and experiencing anxiety. I remember our last meeting vividly. My coach, as I liked to call her, looked at me and said, "I think we're done here." I replied, "Sounds good. So, what's wrong with me? What's your diagnosis?" She looked at me and said, "You're just learning how to get in touch with your feelings." I was shocked. I asked, "That's it?" Yep.

I shouldn't have been surprised. It's not like my dad was a professor of emotional intelligence. He, like the men in his life and his culture, simply did what men did. All good, except my range of emotional understanding was limited, and would be for years.

As a safety mechanism, I also learned to limit my emotional involvement as a career firefighter. It was never the case that I (or we) could show up to all the emergency calls and become emotionally involved with patients. It wouldn't have been survivable. I did what I imagine most firefighters do: I shut down my emotions when dealing with sick, injured, and mortally wounded people to protect myself. Then, ideally, when I left shift in the morning and went home, I would magically turn my emotions back on.

Right...

I think about this:

It's 2010, and life being what life is, and given these landscapes we walk, I spent time with orphans in Eastern Europe. My wife and children were there too. Orphans, on par, have a limited emotional vocabulary. Same as firefighters, I guess. You simply do what you have to do to survive.

Orphans, in an orphanage, tend to quickly notice anger. Imagine me sitting with orphans and showing them feelings flashcards, and together we're learning about feelings, making faces, and learning postures to discover new emotions—more than just anger. I can imagine it, because I did it. I learned too.

Life marches on, and in January of 2015, I was in the desert at a weeklong mindfulness retreat designed for those who worked in high stress operational environments, like fire, law enforcement, military, and intelligence. At this retreat, I learned to name and sit with various emotions and understand how they showed up in my body. For example, when I am joyful, I feel it in my chest with warmth and lightness. But even during this fairly advanced mindfulness retreat, the range of emotions we learned to work with was limited: happiness, sadness, anger, joy, anxiety, and maybe a few others.

Ever since that particular retreat, I've meditated. It stuck with me because it was healing. Call it mindfulness if you like. But also call it prayer, or silence. I am able to—actually, I *embrace* sitting in silence and going deep within my inner landscape.

Have I circumnavigated this inner globe? Perhaps, but doubtful. To think, some folks travel the world and never take the time to travel their inner landscape: their spirit, their heart, their will—that blip of light hiding behind their chest wall, filled with light, heat, and breath.

Maybe, if we travel inside, we find God.

Where am I going with all this waxing? Just here: I have never in my life experienced the emotional complexity and dark, painful inner landscape that I have encountered over the last several months in the aftermath of Cooper's death.

When I taught high school religious studies for a short season of life, I once introduced freshmen students to a basic meditation (centering prayer). Students sat in silence for a few minutes. In that short time, I had three students in the hallway crying because they couldn't sit with the intensity of what they found, what they came face-to-face with, in their inner place—the deep place, where the coins are. The silence and inner landscape unnerved them. They left the coins on the bottom of the pond and quickly came up for air.

You know those indigenous pearl divers who dive to the bottom of a sea cove and spend three relaxed minutes exploring the depths? Yeah, it was not that.

Today, I can sit with the myriad grief emotions within me. I can't, however, easily name these emotions. I can't untangle them. The emotional complexity of child loss, especially in the early weeks, is intense and very, very difficult. I couldn't sit with them.

If you'll bear with me, I envision a thin thread of light running through the center of my body, top to bottom. The part of the strip of light that runs behind my chest, the part in my heart, pulsates—with my breath, with the silence, with the heartbeat of life under the ground that nobody hears but is there. At this place, where the light pulsates, the Universe took a giant ball of emotional complexity and tossed it in.

A spiritual pitcher gathered up all the emoticons, balled them into a spiritual baseball, and threw a 105 mph fastball at my chest. The pitcher said, *"Here, sit with this."*

During the first three weeks after Cooper's death, I walked around the house, probably in shock, muttering, "This is fucking terrible. This is fucking terrible..." My wife would say, *"Stop saying that, it doesn't even begin to describe this."* She was right, of course. It didn't. But I didn't know what else to say.

Words failed. I tried: sorrow, hurt, tragedy, sadness, negation, vacuum, tears, shattered, micro-atomic bomb, dark season of the soul, memories had, memories that will not be had, fear, despair, depression, anger, confusion, emptiness, nausea, pain.

All that and more, pressed together like a snowball. Big ol' hands of the Universe packing a special grief meatball, seasoning it with all the things.

Today, as I sit in the library, I can say honestly, I am okay. I can say, I am going to continue to be okay, and I will make it. I can say with confidence, I am not going to forget my son, which, oddly enough, was my earliest fear.

I want those who have recently lost a child, and those who will lose a child, to know: it's going to be hard, you're never going to be the same, but you will make it—and you will not forget your child.

As time moves on, I begin to remember things. Still fragmented...

I spend a lot of time outdoors when I'm home, in the yard, or on walks. Now, I see the Cessna 172 planes overhead and I think of

Cooper and smile. These planes have been overhead for months, but just now I'm noticing them. Cooper, I imagine, is literally above me, looking down from his Cessna. Before Cooper died, he was taking flying lessons and would literally fly directly over our house.

Cooper was very intrigued with crows when he moved to the Midwest. He would set silver coins on the fence post in the backyard for them. Crows are very intelligent birds, and it doesn't surprise me that Cooper would be captivated by them. Lately, without fail, when I take the dogs out in the backyard in the morning, there are three crows making a racket above me in the trees. I smile and think of Cooper. Of course, these crows have been there for months, but only now am I noticing them, and I can remember Cooper fondly without the full thrust of the pain of grief.

A Cooper's Hawk often sits on a low branch in the backyard. I smile. Has it always been there?

I'm enjoying my new part-time job. Three days a week, morning and afternoon, I drive near the site where Cooper took his life. I say my prayers, I lift my boy up, and I pray for all my family and friends. I know Cooper's death is hard on me and my wife; we will never be the same. But I also know Cooper's death is hard on his brothers, sister, extended family, and friends. We all hurt.

Life has certainly been fragmented.

Near our house, there's a Catholic Church. Before Mass, Saturday and Sunday, the bells toll. Historically, the church bells tolled for Mass, yes, but also for funerals.

John Donne, English poet (1572–1631), writes in his poem *For Whom the Bell Tolls*, when the church bells ring for a funeral, there is no reason for us to ask, "For whom do the church bells toll?" We don't need to ask "who" died, because the answer is: we did. The bells, they toll for thee.[1]

Donne is arguing that we're all connected. He's saying a thousand, million threads of spirit bind us tightly together into a common humanity.

As I say, the smallest indivisible unit in the Kingdom of God is... two. Not one.

When Cooper died, we all died a little death. This complexity of emotions, this fragmentation, and yes, even this healing, we're in it together. And, we're going to be okay, it's going to be okay.

Yes, the bells, they toll for thee.

grief as negation

G od is most often described in the positive. By this, I mean positive attributes. For example, people describe God as joyful, loving, all-knowing, ever-present, creative, and merciful. These are positive attributes of God.

Some religious traditions, however, prefer to understand God in the negative. Not as in God being negative, but in accepting that there are many things we don't know about God and will never know. For example, in the negative, we might say God is unknowable, indescribable, and beyond logic and comprehension. Negative theology accepts that God is beyond what we can put into words and that anything we can say about God ultimately falls far short of His significance.

I think both a positive and negative theological understanding of God is important. But that's not my focus here today.

Grief, like God, is something I have tried to describe in the positive. I attempt, in very human fashion, to give words to my experience of pain and loss. I use terms like despair, sorrow, shattered, etc.

I am beginning to think, though, that the best description of grief is to understand it in the negative.

So often, when I encounter parents who learn that we have lost a child, their first words to us are usually something along the lines of, "I'm so sorry for your loss. I cannot even imagine."

I usually say to them, with love, "No, you cannot imagine it, and you do not want to." This language, "I cannot even imagine," is an expression of grief in the negative.

Losing a child is the experience of pain and loss that is incomprehensible to those who have not been through it.

I want to explore this idea through a few examples.

Long ago, I read an intriguing article about intelligence agency black ops sites. I don't remember all the details, but the concept was that these sites were showing up on heat maps as negations, as empty spaces. All around a particular geographic area, there was heat activity, except in certain places. The negation—what was not there—revealed more about what was there than the positive attributes of heat and light. The absence (black on a heat map) told a bigger story than the presence of activity.

In philosophy, there's a branch called "phenomenology." It's one of my favorite branches because it goes deep. Simplifying a bit, phenomenology attempts to study what's not there, what's not seen. I remember a particular homework assignment where I described an orphanage entirely by what was not seen or observed.

Let's say I'm at work and a friend, a coworker, shows up. Normally, I notice what's there. This is normal, right? A smile, a friendly exchange of pleasantries, their dress, mannerisms, behavior. I see things, I notice.

Phenomenology asks, what is behind what we see, what's not there? Interestingly enough, as I write this, I think of Cooper. Perhaps I should have more frequently considered what I wasn't seeing. What were the possibilities?

Over the last several months, I have been regularly attending a The Compassionate Friends support group for grieving parents. I find incredible value in this group.

Why?

The main reason I find value in our group, I think, is because I am instantly and automatically bonded with those who have experienced the negation, the empty space, the loss of a child. These parents can look beyond how I show up at meetings and see the negative spaces in my life and spirit. Not only do they see my empty places, they understand them.

I know, they know. They know, I know.

At our last The Compassionate Friends meeting, a friend, a grieving mother, said through tears, "I miss the future." Her words struck me to the heart. I understood.

In losing our son, Cooper, we miss out on his future. We won't see the goals he would have achieved, the relationships he would have had, the possibility of a wedding, of grandchildren, his future laughter, holidays together, time at the oak table breaking bread, craft beers together at the pub, nights on the couch watching sports, and so much more.

I miss the future, too.

Notice, our pain is shared around negation—what will not be there in the future.

During this same meeting, a father, another friend, shared his thoughts about the poem *The Road Not Taken* by Robert Frost.

I'm not sure I understood his thoughts entirely, but I took something from his sharing.

As a father, I am moving through life with my children. As they grow up, we are all walking together on the same road, physically. Naturally, as children age, we come to a point where it's time to let go and let them take their own path. They break off from the common road we're all on and they diverge.

While they take a new road to physically travel, we are still walking forward together in spirit. They are on their road, I am on mine, but I know they are there, on their path. My heart and mind are tracking their journey. I am still walking "with" them in spirit and praying for them.

With Cooper, my spirit knows he's no longer even on the road. We were walking together, and now, I walk on my path with my wife, and his path is empty. There's no Cooper on the diverged road.

Notice the negation.

My attempt here is to give some broader understanding of grief by understanding it as a negation, an emptiness, rather than an expression of what we observe.

Here's one more example: three years ago, I had a bone marrow biopsy performed on the iliac crest of my pelvis, on my backside. After numbing the area, the doctor inserted a large-gauge needle into the hollow of my bone and drew marrow out with a suction/vacuum.

I will never forget the feeling of the vacuum pulling marrow out of my bones. I almost passed out, and I told the doctor I was fading. I felt nauseous and ill. I've never experienced that feeling in my life, and I never want to again.

Losing Cooper is something like the spiritual equivalent of that medical procedure. A large-gauge needle inserted into my soul and sucking out some of the spiritual marrow.

Pulling the breath from my lungs.

Like the Dementors in *Harry Potter* pulling on the soul.

This is why death hurts, especially the death of a child. Cooper occupied time and space and filled our lives with positive attributes. Now, nothing.

The question I have for life, for the Universe, is: What now fills this empty space? Or, as a grieving father, do I now accept that the rest of my life will be lived with an aching hollowness at the core of my being?

In life, it's obvious that there is a natural order of things, or there should be. Beyond the aching hole of losing a child, my biological-spiritual system is abundantly aware that the natural order has been disrupted.

Consider this quote:

> *"The death of a child is one of the most painful events that an adult can experience and is linked to complicated/traumatic grief reactions (Prigerson et al., 1999). For parents, the dissolution of the attachment relationship with the child elicits severe anxiety and other negative emotions associated with loss (Bowlby, 1980). Parents might also experience guilt about having been unable to protect the child (Gilbert, 1997). Furthermore, because the death of a child defies the expected order of life events, many parents experience the event as a challenge to basic existential assumptions (Wheeler, 2001)."* —National Center for Biotechnology Information [1]

The death of a child does challenge basic existential assumptions. If the profound challenges of child loss can strike me, what else does life have in store for me? Is there another boogeyman just around the corner? How safe is this place? Can I trust life? Can I trust... God?

Losing a child makes me question the basic order of creation.

I think I know why I have not been angry with God. I'm not angry with God because, after all, I'm not even sure God exists.

Do you feel me? Can you understand?

To those who have lost a child and still have faith, I am watching, listening, and learning.

6 months
April 8, 2024
By Victoria, Coop's mom

Six months ago, our lives took a devastating turn that we never saw coming—a turn that no parent should ever have to endure. On October 8, 2023, our youngest son, Cooper, passed away. He was 23.

I have contemplated whether I would ever even post this on Facebook, but I decided I would, because I knew questions about pictures would come up at some point. Some of you have known this for six months, and others will learn today. There are no words to explain our devastation, and if you haven't lost a child, you will never understand, and we truly hope you never do.

Kelly has blogged about his grief journey. For me, I now just go through the motions each day. My heart is heavy and broken, and my brain just cannot accept not seeing my youngest son again.

If you see me, I do my best to keep it together in public. I took five weeks off from school, and now school is a welcome distraction for my mind. The weekends are a different story. I relive our last Saturday, when I thought things were okay, to Sunday morning when I found out it never would be again.

Anyone who knows me well knows that our family of six is everything to me. To have a piece missing is just too much for a mom's brain. I will forever hope that he will appear at the door, even though I know that can't happen.

Party of Six

I am not okay, nor will I ever be, but we do appreciate people reaching out to us, telling us they are thinking of us and Cooper. Think of Cooper, tell stories about him, look at his pictures, ask me what he was like—I will cry, as I can't talk about him without doing that—but he was such an incredibly smart, caring person. It will never make sense. But please, say his name.

Love,

Victoria

~

kindness

Hi Friends,

I am due for an update to let you know what's been going on. Many of you are vested in our well-being, and you have been praying for our family. I want to thank you for your prayers. I accept your special grace. I see God through you. True story.

Were it not for you, I would sit in the screaming silence of a silent God. For the record, if I were God, I would let you know I was with you. You would feel me and hear from me. When you screamed out in pain, I would respond. You would say, "I know God exists because He is with me as an experienced reality."

But who is to say it is not your prayers lifting my nose above the waterline day by day? On those days when the water is choppy, perhaps it is your beautiful palms lifted in five seconds of prayer that raise me two to three inches for the day. Brother, sister, two to three inches is life when your nose is splashing in the waterline on a choppy day. Keep praying, please.

Lord, I don't believe; help my unbelief. Lord, I don't believe, but

I accept the prayers of my beloved believers. Lord, Your peek-aboo when people most need You is unbecoming.

As it is, I'm at the local pub, cruising. I rode my mountain bike over and I am drinking a fine locally brewed lager. Well, now I am several craft beers deep. Who's counting?

Notwithstanding these beautiful hops, it's been a beautiful day. The birds are singing, it's 74 degrees, moderately cloudy, and the wind is pleasant—not that rascally crap-wind that irritates me so.

As I sit here at the local pub, a good friend, a neighbor, came over to have a beer with me. That's funny, let's call it a few beers.

We were chopping it up, talking about all the things—except my son, Cooper. I didn't want to talk about Cooper because why would I drop this on another man if I didn't need to? No need to. My friend and neighbor didn't know.

My wife shows up and meets us both after her workday, and she mentions something about Cooper. We briefly share the story with my friend. My friend then shares from the deep place, where the coins are, the place where most people come up for air, and where this friend does not; he shares, hard.

His story resonates.

It's beautiful and sad, and tears fill my eyes. They fill my friend's eyes. They fill my wife's eyes. We're all f**king crying, at the local pub, on a beautiful day, with the pleasant winds.

Before proceeding, it's important, I think, to tell you about the kindest thing that has happened to me, by a stranger.

We were in Eastern Europe, my wife and I. Summer, 2010. The point of our being in Eastern Europe is best saved for another day, but suffice it to say, we were doing God's work. We got beat up, badly, spiritually. I can attest, there are demons that roam this earth. We met them, and they are demonic. What shall I say? We had our asses handed to us. Pure spiritual beatdown, top to bottom.

We left Eastern Europe with our tails between our legs, beat down, humbled, hurt. We flew home through Amsterdam.

We were in Amsterdam for a 12-hour layover through the early morning hours. I was sleeping on the hard floor of the airport using my backpack as my pillow, in the fetal position, my two hands in the prayer position between my knees. As I slept, I vaguely remember a person walking over to me and laying a blanket over me. It was not a dream, they did. A person walked over to me and laid a blanket over me as I slept on the ground, and then walked away. To this day, I don't know who this person was.

I love you, person. You remain with me.

I don't know why, but today this registers as the kindest thing a stranger has done for me. I remember it vividly.

Back to tonight. As I sat at our table with my wife and friend, talking suicide and loss, tears filled my eyes. Nothing really unusual about this; it happens. Except tonight, a retired law enforcement officer from another table, whom I did not know, came over and said, "Looks like you need a hug." And this big, bearded man hugged me. And we stood there and hugged, silent, for a long time.

Ah yes, the silent God. I see You now, not so unbecoming. I stand corrected.

I am telling you now, this is the second kindest thing a stranger has done for me. The kindness shook me.

Who notices things like this? Who gets up out of their chair to come over and hug a stranger in a pub?

Bro.

God?

~

grief fingerprint

May 21, 2024

Today is our daughter's graduation from high school. We are so proud of her and the hard work she has put in over these last four years. Grace, a.k.a., Little Miss Sunshine (LMS), has had an amazing journey, she has a beautiful story to tell, and you would all be very proud of her. Here's to her new beginnings!

It's also bittersweet because we know how much Cooper loved his sister and how happy he would be for her today. I pray he is somewhere up there, smiling down on us.

Sunshine's brothers, her future sister-in-law, and Nanny and Poppy from Arizona are all in town. We're all here, and we've been celebrating. Trying to celebrate. Doing the best we can to celebrate.

In 2017, I was in Bozeman, MT, having dinner with my cousin "KK" at a local eatery. During dinner, KK explained to me that one of her favorite things in life is celebrating. She loves to celebrate all of life's occasions. I thought this was cool, but to be honest, I had never thought much about celebrations, and as a general rule, I don't tend to celebrate very well.

Yay, you scored a touchdown, awesome, that's your job, now get off the field. What does Jocko say? "Nobody cares, work harder."

This idea of celebrating, as shared by my cousin, is on my mind more frequently these days. It's very easy to be consumed by grief and thoughts of Cooper—all the time. After the loss of our son, celebrating birthdays now seems like a bigger deal to me. Our oldest son just celebrated his 29th birthday, and it's a big deal, worthy of celebration.

I am finding, though, that celebrating is not so easy. I am having to be very intentional to embrace Sunshine's accomplishments and focus on her, this special moment, her success, and her commencement this evening. I am surprised by how hard it is to stay focused on the good happening right now, here, today.

I am trying to say: our daughter's graduation is highlighting how difficult it is to celebrate these days, even though I want to and I have a greater appreciation for it.

The last time our boys, daughter-in-law, and Nanny and Poppy were in town was in the immediate aftermath of Cooper's death. What we are discovering during this visit for Grace's graduation is that the body does indeed keep the score.[1] There are triggers.

Even though we are "celebrating," it's hard not to notice the gaping hole of Cooper not being here. We all feel it and sense it. Our bodies are saying to us, "Hey, the last time you all were together, things were not good."

During these few days together, with family in town, I am also realizing how important my daily routines have been to my healing process. I'm not in routine right now, and I feel it. My shadow is long these last few days.

Truth be told, I have felt good over the last few months. Smaller shadow, less casting. I have become aware that things are going to be okay. Not great, but okay. I have genuinely sensed some level of healing taking place in my life.

I went back to work part-time in March, working within community risk reduction. Four weeks ago, I was at a public school delivering risk reduction curriculum to second graders. In one scenario, I was working with a small group of students, teaching them how to call 9-1-1 on a real phone with a 9-1-1 training application installed on it. It's a pretty cool, high-fidelity learning device for second graders.

This one little girl said her name into the phone, and the phone misheard her and began to call her "Pandoras." This little girl let out the most authentic laughter I have ever heard, and she could not stop laughing. Her laughter was infectious. Before I knew it, I too was laughing. Authentically, from the deep place, bubbling up to my face, I was laughing. My spine was shaking. Real laughter.

We finished with the group, and I was standing, waiting for the next group, outside, in the sun, on a beautiful day, watching a Cooper's Hawk. I remember thinking to myself, *I am healing*. I said to myself, *that* laughter just now was genuine. It registered with me that it was the first time I had authentically laughed, from my soul, since Cooper had died. I think it was a good sign.

Back to all my family in town. With the triggers firing from the last time we were all together—genuine trauma—and with my routine out of balance these last few days, it's given me pause to realize how raw I still am. I'm not healing as much as I thought I was.

Remember, I don't expect to be fully healed from the loss of Cooper, but I do expect that healing will take place. In resilience studies, there is recovery, adaptation, and transformation. In general, I think society, maybe family and friends, expect bereaved parents to recover at some point in time. You know, to "bounce back." To get back to who we were, and rather quickly. What really happens is transformation. We will not be the same people we were, and whoever the new person we will become through transformation will take a long time. Years. At least five, likely twenty or more.

I will outlive my life before I become the new me.

In the days after Cooper's death, I ran into my neighbor while I was walking the dogs. She works in mental health. She gave me sage advice that has stayed with me. I remember our conversation vividly. It was early, around 7 a.m., and we were talking across the street, as we both had our dogs and mine was being a barking nuisance. She said, *everyone is going to grieve at different paces and in different ways, and you just have to accept it.*

I see it with my family, with my children, how they all are grieving differently and in their own unique way. I have come to call this a "grief fingerprint." I think we all have our own grief fingerprint, and we are going to grieve in our own way, at our own pace, and nobody's grief fingerprint will look like another's.

I read three books immediately after Cooper died, I read everything I could get my hands on in Cooper's iPhone, and I joined The Compassionate Friends. I did not do formal counseling. My wife, meanwhile, hasn't finished a single book, hasn't read any of Cooper's text messages, and she cuddles his hoodie at night. Different fingerprints.

I can see how different grief fingerprints could create challenges in relationships, including marriages. If a couple starts to diverge too significantly in how they are processing grief, and their timelines are very different, it's bound to create some stress in the relationship. This is why I think it's important to know this is likely to happen and to simply "embrace the suck."

I am grateful our loss has tended to bond our marriage closer. We are very kind to each other, and we give each other wide berth to process and deal in our own unique way. We are, for better or worse, trauma-bonded.

The other thing I am aware of these past few days is that I find it difficult to compartmentalize my emotions. Happy bleeds over into grief. I am happy and joyful for my daughter. I want to lean in hard and celebrate her special day, and yet my joyful emotions get confused in me with grief and sadness, the big gaping hole in my chest, the emptiness, the negative space of hurt, good ol' Melancholy Man.

Does this resonate with others who are grieving?

My emotions don't have distinct names and places inside me, as they used to. Now they're just emotions. Said another way, all of my emotions, even the good ones, somehow have a tendency to anchor back to grief and the loss of Cooper.

I think with intentionality, I can work on this, but it is an observation.

As a kid growing up, I remember learning about the Kubler-Ross five stages of grief model. I suppose, initially, I had the idea that grieving the loss of Cooper would be something like this model —five stages. I thought, I guess, that I would move from one stage of grief to the next, sort of self-actualizing up the pyramid, like Maslow's Hierarchy.

I would take anger and bargaining with God to be good signs that I was coming around, working my way through the five stages of grief.

I am not suggesting the Kubler-Ross five stages of grief model is applicable to the loss of a child. What I am saying is that, up to now, I would have assumed it was. And I think most of society, rightly or wrongly, would apply this grief model to a bereaved parent.

Seven months after Cooper's death, it's now very clear to me the Kubler-Ross five stages of grief model is not a good framework for mapping the grief journey following the loss of a child, or a brother, or a grandson.[2] In my experience, it's not applicable. Maybe don't throw the baby out with the bathwater, but I am not inclined to use this model as a touchstone for navigating the grief of losing a child.

While I was with my Compassionate Friends group earlier this month, we were talking about the impulses that come over us in the early months of grieving; in the early years of grieving. You know, like giving the bird to the world, selling your belongings, and becoming a nomad. Alcohol, drugs, promiscuity, risk-taking, anger. All the things.

The impulses are there, for sure. Because who cares now, you've just experienced the worst thing ever, so screw it, go for broke.

You can't hurt me now, or something like that. I understand this line of thought.

But that said, I maintain that we have an obligation, a duty, to grieve in a healthy manner the best we can. If we, as a family, can all abide by this, then the style and pace of our grieving doesn't matter. We can give each other wide berth.

The truth is, our family is tender, raw, and very exposed. I can see it's going to take serious and mindful navigation to keep us all together, healing, and kind to one another over the next few years.

I'm drawn to the voyage of Ernest Shackleton on the ship *Endurance*. All of his men survived that trip, intact, despite the incredible challenges they faced.

That's how I feel as a husband, father, son, brother, and friend right now. I am asking myself, *how do I lead my family best during this very tumultuous season of life and ensure everyone survives, thrives, and comes out on the other side of the valleys, intact?*

Perhaps it will only be by the grace of God. I am convinced, if God shows up, it will be through people acting on His behalf. I don't expect to encounter God. I expect, I suppose, to encounter God through good people acting in His name.

Friends, these last few days of having family in town to celebrate Sunshine's graduation have made it clear to me that this is going to be a long journey through many valleys. There will be danger.

Yea, though I walk through the valley of the shadow of death, I will fear no evil, for You are with me; Your rod and Your staff, they comfort me. Surely—surely—goodness and mercy will follow me all the days of my life. If Cooper is in the house of the Lord, then yes, I do want to dwell there forever.

how ought a man to grieve the loss of his child?

May 23, 2024

How Ought a Man to Grieve the Loss of His Child?[1]
Firefighting is inherently dangerous and remains primarily a man's work. Yes, women are increasingly joining the U.S. fire service, but to this day, the profession is overwhelmingly represented by men.

I am a man, and I have spent my adult life in the fire service. I lived, moved, and found my being among men. Grown men. Aggressive men who channeled their behavior toward protecting life and property in local communities. Compassionate men who rarely worked alone.

There is a biological predisposition and learned behavior firefighters have that I describe as "John Wayne-ing" it. This manifests as fierce determination, grit, problem-solving, and not asking for help. These are behaviors many men learn and are naturally predisposed to.

But what happens when we, as men, experience the loss of our child?

On October 8, 2023, we lost our 23-year-old son, Cooper, to suicide. I don't like writing that word. It pains me deeply, yet it is the ground truth. I cannot undo it.

A micro-atomic bomb was dropped on our house, on our lives. I dropped to my knees as the air was sucked out of me. I couldn't stand, and I couldn't breathe. Yes, I cried. I wailed. I still cry.

I remember many of the fires I fought. I was never alone; I was always with a crew of firefighters. We practiced the buddy system. We worked in pairs of at least two. If we went into a fire together, we came out together. It was that simple. As the firefighters say in *Backdraft*, "If you go, we go." Meaning, your brother or sister firefighter is not going to leave you in the fire if something happens to you.

Cooper

In a fire, in a fire station, and in the fire department, firefighters practice a lot of togetherness. Tough times, responding to tough calls, require "tight togetherness." In a small fire, for example, firefighters can work off the hose line away from each other but within verbal communication range. In a complex, difficult fire, firefighters have a hand on each other's back and do not leave each other. The proximity is dialed to the level of physical touch.

Immediately after my son died, my brother flew into town to be with me. He slept on the floor next to the couch where I slept for four nights. We got up at night a few times, cried, and hugged each other. He chose to enter the fire with me, and we practiced a lot of tight togetherness. He had a hand on my shoulder. The immediacy of Cooper's death required this level of proximity.

I know of a man who has lost a son. He is grieving deeply. He lives near a lake, and he has chosen to focus on his dogs, fishing, and solitude. He's "John Wayne-ing" it.

I respect this. I respect this man. I honor him. Who am I to suggest how a man ought to grieve? If we are truth-telling, I could very easily be this man. I could check out, thumb my nose at all the things, and live in solitude. I do not think I would be wrong. Perhaps I should do this.

CJ, Carse, Cooper, Seaport Village, San Diego, CA

Despite this impression, my history and behavioral conditioning in the fire service run deep within me, and I want to be with my brother. I don't want to be alone in my grief. I do not want to walk alone. I know that this is a complex, difficult fire, and I need to be working with a crew.

I talk to my wife, my mom, my children, my brother, and my Compassionate Friends frequently. I want to talk about my son, what happened, and how I am feeling. I write. I walk. I breathe. I ground. I lean into tight togetherness and work as a team to help me make sense of this gaping, painful hole in my chest.

To be fair, I think a man needs time alone—time to process, time in the woods with his dogs, fishing the lake. We lived in the mountains for several years, and this resonates with me. As I like to say, we may need to hole up in a Nepalese cave and drink yak's milk with the shamans to begin to make sense of this tragedy.

A man needs this for a season. Maybe a few seasons. There is no shame in this.

Still, I want to call men to tight togetherness following the loss of their child. When the fire is complex, hot, dynamic, and dangerous, I know it is the time and place to practice tight togetherness. Hands on shoulders.

Knowing men the way I do, especially after working in high-risk operational environments for most of my life, it could be that only other men who "know" are able to talk with a grieving man who has lost a child. This may be the signal that gets through the noise.

Cooper

I remember a counselor coming to the fire station after a tragic call our crew had responded to. The counselor had never worked with firefighters and didn't know a thing about fire service culture. We ran the counselor off; he had no credibility.

If a man has not lost a child and offers to help me, despite his best intentions, it would land flat. I would run him off. To talk to me about the loss of a child, you need to show up with credibility. You need to have lost a child.

The mantra of The Compassionate Friends is, "We need not walk alone." In the fire service, this is a lived reality. Firefighters don't work alone. As the saying goes, "If you go, we go."

Men, how ought we to grieve the loss of our child? With rugged determination and grit, certainly, but also, not alone. My humble admonition is this: do not do it alone. Go in together, come out together. Lace your solitude with compassionate family and friends who "know" and will put a hand on your shoulder and not leave you during the darkest night of your soul.

Especially in the loss of a child, practice tight togetherness. You need not walk alone.

hedgehogs
June 10, 2024

F riends, I found a letter Cooper wrote when he was 13 years old. It provides some insight into our beautiful boy. It highlights his love for animals, and particularly hedgehogs. I'm not really sure why, but Cooper loved hedgehogs.

Hedgehogs are Cooper's spirit animal.

This short letter captures Cooper's inquisitiveness. He was certainly a smart boy, he had lots of questions.

How many 13 year olds were calling out the internet for accuracy, back in 2013!?

Anyway, many of you have mentioned you like reading things about Cooper. I was looking for something else in my files today and came across this. It made me smile.

Enjoy!

Ps- the doctor's name is not John Doe. Also, Cooper had proper salutation for his letter, I shortened it up for simplicity. I have not made any corrections otherwise, the letter is as written.

Cooper James

August 2nd, 2013

Dear Dr. John Doe,

Hi, my name is Cooper James and I have a few questions for you regarding hedgehogs. I'm thirteen years old and ever since I visited a hedgehog at the local zoo I have found that I would love to have one as a pet. After researching a little bit about them, I discovered that they were officially "legal" in Arizona however you have to have a permit that is very difficult to obtain. I haven't found out the actual requirements for this permit but I have read online it is "virtually impossible to obtain" (Hedgehog Central).

So one question I have is what are the actual requirements, and why, if Hedgehog Central was correct, are these permits so hard to obtain? I've also found online that hedgehogs were illegal here because they have highly contagious foot and mouth disease. Now this is something I understand but from my research these diseases are typically only found on hedgehogs sold from pet stores. I believe that if hedgehogs were illegal to sell in pet stores, and only from highly credited and certified breeders then these diseases would not cause a problem.

Please note that all of my facts are based off research from the Internet so I might not be correct in everything I say. That's why I'm sending this letter to get more information on the topic. You can contact back through the return address or my email ...@gmail.com. Thank you for time and have a nice day!

Sincerely, Cooper James

freezing
June 14, 2024

When a person encounters a stressful or tough situation, I think there are three responses available: fight, flee, or freeze.

As a Generation X'er, I grew up with my fair share of fighting. The bigger the party, the bigger the fights. Some of my readers will remember those fights well. We were not malicious; we just ran hard, and fighting seemed normal when I was in high school.

Of course, I then spent a career in the fire service "fighting" fires.

Fighting—a fight response—is not new to me. I have neural pathways for this response.

Many years ago, while living in Southern Arizona, my wife and I were walking with our golden retriever, Winky, to the bus stop to pick up one of the kids. It was a sunny, marginally cloudy day, and there had been a little bit of lightning, but nothing significant. As we were getting close to the bus stop, a bolt of lightning flashed down and struck a street pole about 50 yards away from us. Without even thinking, the dog and I ran 100 yards down the road, leaving my wife standing there alone. She froze, and I fled with the dog.

We laughed about it later. It's still funny to me. My wife learned she should never count on me to save her in a thunderstorm with lightning bolting down. She's clearly on her own.

The point is, I fled. My system kicked in, and I ran, with my dog, 100 yards down the road without thinking.

There are many instances in my past where I've fled. Again, not a new response for me. Thinking back on my professional life, particularly in administrative settings, I can recall "fleeing" uncomfortable situations.

What's new for me today, in my grief after the loss of Cooper, is freezing.

Cooper's birthday was in early June, and I froze as the day came and went. I think I froze on Thanksgiving and Christmas, too.

When these significant dates come—the "firsts"—I have difficulty figuring out how to respond, what to do, and how to best honor my son, who is no longer here.

There's nothing to fight, nothing to flee, so I just clam up and don't do anything monumental. I freeze.

I have read in the grief literature that the best way to tackle firsts, like the first Thanksgiving, Christmas, New Year's, birthdays, etc., without your child is to plan ahead for what you're going to do. They say you need to get ahead of the curve.

This sounds nice in theory, but for me, I freeze and then let a grief wave wash over me for a day. I do get emotional on these days. These emotions are not as complex or as strong as they once were, but they're still challenging to work through, even if only for a day.

For Cooper's birthday, we got burritos and Mexican beer. I turned my hat backward, the way Cooper always wore his. I turned my hat around, ate a burrito, and drank a Dos Equis lager. I toasted Cooper.

As I said, frozen. That's as far as I could get.

There's a question I am asked a lot, and it's a question I would have been in the habit of asking others before, and the question is, "How many children do you have?"

This question initially causes me to freeze. I am getting better at answering it, but it takes me a minute to calibrate, to breathe. This question has made me realize how direct it is, and perhaps unsettling. It's a question I no longer ask others. I would love to hear about someone's children, but I will let them tell me about their children without me asking how many they have.

When asked, I always answer, "I have four children." Because I do. It just so happens that one of them is dancing on pinheads with the angels these days.

Months ago, I couldn't think, remember, or organize very well. Today, I am better. Maybe not 100%, but I am cognitively functioning much better. Approaching normal, on most days.

Months ago, the complexity of emotions within me and washing over me was so tough and challenging to deal with. Today, my emotions and feelings have calmed, and I have much more emotional balance in day-to-day life.

Physically, I'm okay, but I'm probably drinking more than I normally would. I'm okay with this, for now. I'm not drinking nearly as much coffee as I was eight months ago.

Spiritually, something is awakening. I am wrestling with questions, and I no longer want to throat punch God. I am in the arena; I am praying and I am meditating.

And yet, I still freeze on those special days, the "firsts," when I simply don't know what else to do, when the reality—the full weight—of losing my son lands on me, for a day.

Fighting is easy. Fleeing is easy.

Freezing, caught between fighting and fleeing in the nervous system, is new space for me, and it's difficult.

As Father's Day approaches, I have a plan—freeze. Just numb up and let the wave crash down...

∾

The alter they want me to heal at is in church.

The alters I am actually healing at in this season of life are DJ turntables and pub tables.

There are others, but these serve as representative examples.

Seasons of life. But where do we find God, and rugged hope, and peace for our eternal souls? You know what they say, "it depends."

May I suggest the sacraments?

> Sacrament of Silence,
>
> Sacrament of Writing,
>
> Sacrament of Nature,
>
> Sacrament of Reading,
>
> Sacrament of Tears,
>
> Sacrament of Breath,
>
> Sacrament of Dogs,
>
> Sacrament of Walking,
>
> Sacrament of Music,
>
> Sacrament of Family.

And so on, and so on...

Mix it up, find what works for you, experiment, apply a growth mindset. Nothing ventured, nothing gained.

Be in the arena. The deed is all.

Pray to God to stir up your heart and rekindle the magic, but don't grovel.

wrecked

When Cooper graduated from high school, he wanted to go to Puerto Peñasco (Rocky Point), Mexico, with 18 friends. I was okay with this, provided there would be at least some parental supervision. So, I went with another father, Jason. We stayed in a different hotel, away from the kids. We weren't there so much as supervisors but more as support in case the kids needed help.

As it turned out, Jason and I had a great time. In the mornings, we would kick our feet up on the balcony, drink coffee, and watch several walks of shame pass by below us. "Oh, hi," we would wave and smile. It was quite comical.

There was only one time when we had to "pump the brakes" and play our dad cards. We were at Wrecked at the Reef Cantina, hanging out. Jason and I were with a group of parents from Southern Arizona, eating, drinking, and chatting, when Cooper came up to me to ask a question. He had a JUUL (vape) in his hand and took a long drag, blowing smoke in my face.

He was buzzed and genuinely wasn't being a smartass; he had just lost complete situational awareness. I asked him, "Have you lost your freaking mind?" He looked at me, stunned. "What?" I said, "Dude, you're vaping in front of me!" Cooper was like, "Oh, shit!" A shit-eating grin crossed his face. For those who knew Cooper, you know the smile I'm talking about.

It's funny now, reflecting on this story, and we still laugh about it as a family. Anyway, the kids were pretty liquored up, and they wanted to go into the city. It was already 1 a.m. Jason and I were like, nope. Hell to the nope. Everything you need is right here. Slow your roll, go have fun.

Wrecked, seems appropriate to me these days. The word has the right texture for my life.

Last week, I had the good fortune to attend the National Fire Academy for a week-long course in youth firesetting intervention and prevention. It was a great class, and I met a lot of good people.

Wrecked at the Reef, Rocky Point, Mexico

After the first day of class, our group of 18 (hey, serendipity, interesting number) went to the Command Post Pub to meet and greet and figure out what fun things we wanted to do during the week. I ended up talking to two women, and at some point, I shared that I had lost my son, Cooper. It was Sunday, Father's Day, and I was genuinely having a bit of a tough day. It felt good to share.

One of the women had not lost a child, but she had lost a brother. She shared that she could see her parents struggling but didn't really know what to do or say. She asked me, what should I say? What do I do?

My answer to her was this: honor your brother by living a great life. Let your parents know that you are going to be okay, that you're happy, and that you are going to suck the marrow out of this life and live it for all it's worth. What your parents want more than anything is for you to be healthy, happy, safe, and successful in your own right.

As a parent, I have been wrecked. My wife, too. All of my friends in my The Compassionate Friends group, wrecked. Bereaved parents—wrecked. I'm not suggesting we don't have joy and happiness; we do. But understand, a piece of our soul has been taken, and we don't get it back. We're not whole. Thump my chest, and you will feel the missing piece.

I so did not see this coming in my life.

I may be wrong, but I don't see this wreckage for my children. I know they hurt, and they should, but a piece of their soul has not been taken.

I remember standing with one of my sons over Cooper's body at the funeral home. We were both sobbing tears from a place deep beyond where the coins are. If God is the breath within the breath, then these were the tears within the tears. Our tears were crying.

I put my hand on Carse's shoulder and told him, in truth, "This is the hardest thing you will ever do. Right here, right now."

Imagine my kids, 28, 25, and 18, experiencing this—the valley of the shadow of death. Life laid our Party of Six low—knees to the ground, forehead to the ground, low.

Now they know. My kids know. Now they will bring compassion to others. They are seers and sensers.

What I want to say is: what will bring me the greatest joy in the years remaining in my life is to watch my children do well and live good lives. I don't want them marinating in Cooper's death for too long. I want them to grieve in a healthy manner, at their own pace, yes, but I do want them to find healing and peace and be able to move on. I am confident they will always find ways to honor their brother.

I will stay with the wrecked boat on the reef, but you kids need to go, live, and do well. Crush this motherf**ker called life.

Below is a text message I sent to my oldest sons back in January:

> Hey, boys. I have been going through some of Cooper's things this morning, trying to close a few things out. I went back and read his journal, looking at a few things. In light of that, I wanted to share a few things with both of you. The first thing that stands out to me is that Cooper was doing really well in life, but he didn't see that in himself. He was really hard on himself, held himself to unrealistic expectations. Back when I used to fight fire, there's a saying about standing in the center of the fire. You have to be able to stand in the heat, smoke, and flames and know that even though it doesn't seem like it, you are winning the fire fight. Both of you are doing exceptionally well in life, and I want you to see it, to know it, and to embrace it. You are. You're doing great. Know that. Just keep standing in the center of the fire and have confidence—you are going to win the fire fight. Also, don't be hard on yourselves. Love yourself. Offer yourself kindness, good thoughts, and nice words toward yourself. Don't hold yourself up to unrealistic expectations. Smile. Don't take yourself too seriously. Cooper was too hard on himself and didn't realize how well he was doing. He became unsettled standing in the center of the fire and lost his nerve. Keep your feet on the ground, stay grounded, and keep doing what you're doing. It's working. Love you both, Dad.

Losing a child wrecks you. It should. On all levels, wrecked—physical, emotional, social, spiritual, mental.

But healing does take place. I believe this. It is happening.

I imagine my life as something like Moses. I'm not going to enter the Promised Land. How could I enter the Promised Land without Cooper?

What I hope, though, is to be able to stand on Mount Nebo and watch my sons and daughter living good lives in their Promised Lands. I see smiles on their faces, love in their hearts, and kids scattered everywhere. They know. They are seers and sensers and lovers. They know, but they are living. They live and engage this world with compassionate hearts.

In my heart of hearts, I know and believe I will see my son again. Zero doubt about this. I live today to see my kids do well and to help others. In 2013, I was in Israel and spent time with Zaka Search and Rescue. A rescuer said to me, "If you save one life, it's as if you have saved the whole world." I believe this.

I'm slowly walking toward Mount Nebo, this last third (quarter) of my life. I aim to save one life, maybe many, and then stand on the mountaintop and gaze out at my kids and smile. Then I am going to go see my boy. I can't wait to hug him again.

Wrecked.

ei

June 28, 2024

There's an excellent book in educational circles titled *An Ethic of Excellence: Building a Culture of Craftsmanship with Students*[1] by Ron Berger. It's one of my favorites. The premise of the book, as I understand and remember it, is that children need good models at the start of learning to see and know what excellence looks like.

If you show me a good model, a perfect vision for the future, an ideal end-state, then when I begin my own learning, I will know the direction in which I am heading.

This aligns with my experiences in the fire department in training and learning environments. As instructors and educators, we want to show firefighters at the beginning of training what "right looks like."[2] Once they see the model, they will know what to aim for.

With these thoughts in mind, I want to share an experience I had recently with a mother that provides an exceptional model of excellence in talking to a parent who has lost a child.

I was recently at a public safety event for parents of children aged 0-3. There were several vendor tables set up by different organizations sharing safety messages. One table had a woman discussing the dangers of screen time, social media, and technology for children.

I firmly believe technology and social media played a role in Cooper's death. It's one layer of the suicide onion, at least.

I walked over to the table and began asking questions about her organization, and their findings and message. The conversation unfolded organically, and as time went on, there came an appropriate moment to share openly about my son, Cooper, and his death. I shared that I firmly believed technology played a part in his death.

This woman expressed that she was sorry. She acknowledged that she could not even begin to know what I was experiencing.

This is common language when I meet someone, and my son's death comes up. Usually, it arises when someone in good faith asks me how many children I have. I tell them four, but one of them is no longer with us.

But this woman did something very different. She asked me, over these last many months of grieving, "What have you found most helpful in the grieving process?"

- I told her that breathing, writing, and talking to others about Cooper have been the most helpful.
- Taking time off work was also important for me.
- Joining the local The Compassionate Friends group and meeting other bereaved parents has been helpful.
- Reading a few books on grief and child loss has been helpful.
- Listening to my "Thinking of You, Cooper" soundtrack on long nature walks has been helpful.
- Drinking craft beer at local pubs has been helpful.

- Going back to work has been helpful.
- Having family and friends check in has been helpful.
- Spending time with my dogs has been helpful.
- Going to my little non-programmed Quaker church has been helpful.
- Seeing nature in new and unexpected ways has been helpful.
- Having a daily routine to honor Cooper has been helpful —keeping his candle lit, a light on at night, and opening the window for him in the morning and evening.

After I answered, she then asked me, "What have you found the least helpful?"

What has not been helpful to me are:

- People I thought would really step up but instead stepped away. It seems death is particularly uncomfortable for many people.
- I don't have time for trivial things these days. It used to be I could tolerate ambiguous people and not be bothered by those who were not in my camp or on my side. Today, I don't have time for these folks. If you're not with me or you're against me, we're done. I have far less tolerance for pretending. I don't mean this in a rude or disrespectful way.

I shared some of these things with the woman I was speaking with.

But she continued.

She then asked me, "What's your son's name?" Not in the past tense, but the present tense. "What's his name?" I shared with her, "Cooper."

Then she asked,

"Tell me about Cooper. What was he like?"

A smile spread across my face. Not one person I have met who has learned about my son has ever asked me this question.

So I shared:

Cooper was kind, gentle, and intelligent. He had a wry sense of humor—witty, and you had to be paying attention, or you would miss it. Cooper was a good friend, a soccer player, a budding pilot, and an aerospace engineer. Cooper loved dogs, hedgehogs, and most animals. He smiled gently from the corner of his mouth on the left side. He was introverted and socially shy (awkward).

I shared these thoughts about Cooper with this kind woman.

I can't pretend to speak for all bereaved parents; that wouldn't be fair or appropriate. Yet, this woman modeled excellence in my book.

What is your son's name? Tell me about him.

This is what emotional—and spiritual—intelligence looks and sounds like in real time.

> "Blessed are the merciful,
> for they will be shown mercy.
> Blessed are the pure in heart,
> for they will see God."

thinking of you,
cooper spotify playlist
July 1, 2024

Beginning in October 2023, I slowly started adding songs to my "Thinking of you, Cooper" playlist on Spotify. I like to go on long walks (my Trail of Tears) and listen to this playlist, and usually, the tears flow.

I have developed a new relationship with music these days, a deeper appreciation for how it touches my heart.

You can listen to the playlist here: *Thinking of you, Cooper.*[1] *

When Cooper died, and in the months that followed, I found myself walking and moving in a very, very deep spiritual place. I felt as though I could literally reach out and touch the spiritual world if I wanted to. I mean this sincerely. Out of respect for what's on the other side, the spiritual realm, I never did reach into the void.

I sensed a close connection with *el otro lado* (the other side). Animals and insects took on new meaning. Red foxes, butterflies, dragonflies, robins, cardinals, cranes, and crows all became more than just animals and bugs—they became messengers.

It's funny, but not funny, how in my deepest pain, the spirit world leaned in on me through the natural world.

Riptides have a different meaning to me now, as do wind chimes, dreams, candles, and felt hugs.

I've had three dreams with Cooper in them since he died. My last dream was so real, I woke up crying. It was a good dream, and it lifted me all day. It still lifts me.

I was recently walking the path at a local park when a woman passed me in silence, but with a certain look. She seemed like a spiritual messenger. I wondered if she was an angel. That was my impression. With certain people now, I sit and ponder, I check them out, I wonder: is this a person or an angel?

I have come to realize that the traditional Christian faith I grew up with, and have believed in for most of my adult life, has not provided me with the language and imagery I need to cope with and explain the loss of my son.

If I'm being fair, and I think I should be, it's the second time in my life that I've felt shaken and Jesus was not there. My faith has shifted.

If you're a Christian, I understand that you feel compelled to advocate Jesus to me. I would do the same. Don't be hurt if I share that I have some new territory to explore, which may be outside the bounds of traditional Christianity. I must be true to the muse within me.

I talk to Cooper, his spirit, and I pray for him (his soul) daily. I regularly pray for "the boys" (Cooper, Cas, Kameron, Austin, Cody, and Joshua). I see spirit guides in animals, especially red foxes. I sense Cooper's presence in certain places he used to visit. I can be sitting in the reading room at my house, thinking of Cooper, and the wind chime on the porch will chime at just the right time. It's uncanny.

Despite all the spiritual nuance, life is returning to a baseline. My wife and I are both working, cleaning the house, grocery shopping, working out, reading books, watching television, caring for our children and pets, caring for each other, and doing all the things adults do.

Returning to work part-time has been helpful for my healing process. It has also moved me further away from the deep spiritual place I was in. Perhaps, and I think so, this is a good thing. Being so close to a thin space is good, but these places are not without their inherent dangers.

People often ask, "How are you doing?" My answer is, "I'm okay. I'm not great, and I'm not terrible. I'm okay." And I think, at 10 months in, this is completely acceptable.

I don't cry nearly as often as I used to, but I still do. Just this morning, a good family friend shared a Facebook memory of Cooper's freshman drop-off day at the University of Arizona. Cooper was sitting next to her daughter, and Mama Bear was with Cooper. The picture took my breath away, and the tears welled up.

I was explaining to a friend that I now understand micro-aggressions. To be clear, nobody is being aggressive with me and nobody is intentionally trying to harm me. As I go through each day, I almost always bump up against a conversation related to children. I'm frequently asked how many children I have, or people talk about how difficult their child is being, and I only wish mine were here, etc.

These small wounds add up over the week, and come Friday, it's time to shed some tears. I always feel better after I shed a few. It lets all the funky chemicals out.

Truth be told, I drink more alcohol now than I did before. I don't drink a lot, and I don't have a problem, but I do drink more than I used to. On Fridays, I drink beer and get my buzz on. I'm not sure I do this to numb the pain because I don't feel pain in that way. It's more that I just smile and get happy and can set the grief thoughts behind me for an evening.

I've become good friends with silence and quiet. It's how I best process and grieve. Since I work part-time, my wife works, and our daughter is in school (the boys live outside the home—they are adults), a few days a week it's just me and the puppies. I cherish this time to think slowly, consider, reflect, remember, pray, listen, and try in some way to process this tragic life event. I pay homage to Cooper.

Occasionally, I lean into pity parties. Why me, I wonder? Why am I drinking from this cup? Why didn't it pass over me? My heart and mind move to the mothers in Gaza, and I am quickly humbled, and I forget my pity party.

If you save one life, it's as if you have saved the whole world. Likewise, if you take one life, it's as if you have killed the whole world. No?

We just passed the 10-month mark since we lost Cooper to suicide. I still struggle with wondering why such a beautiful boy, who was seemingly doing so well, self-ejected from life so suddenly and without warning. We don't know why. We know there's no do-over for this one. We don't get a re-do, no take-backs. What's done is done, and oh, so final.

I've perfected my "elevator speech." I say, by rote memory, "We don't exactly know what happened, but it's likely Cooper had undiagnosed clinical depression, which he wasn't receiving treatment for." This seems accurate, but I really don't know. It's a stupid-wild-ass-guess (SWAG).

Does it seem sad that I have to have an elevator speech for relating the loss of my child? It is sad to me. Without the 30-second elevator speech, I would freeze.

I continue to have many questions, but there will be no answers (in this life). I understand this terrible logic.

I have an overwhelming, strong sense that I will see Cooper again on the other side. I know it in my bones, unequivocally.

Zero doubt. Why do I sense this and know it so strongly? I don't know.

I haven't gone back and read any of the blog posts I've written. I write them, read them a few times that day, post them, and I don't look back. I'm not sure I can even go back and read my own writing about what happened. How's that for pain and loss? I remember Cooper, for sure, but I press forward.

I worry about my wife. She's an only child, and she was very close with her father. We lost Poppy Jack to Parkinson's disease in May 2023, and then Cooper, Mama's baby boy, in October 2023. Either one of these is a tough cross to bear on its own, let alone together, in tandem.

I wait in eager expectation for creation to reveal itself and answer some questions. I'm flipping the script. I now more fully understand all the ancient myths where the protagonist is angry with the gods.

A good friend, like a mom to me, frequently checks in with us. She wants us to tell her stories about Cooper on holidays, like the 4th of July. Recently, on August 8th (Cooper died on an 8th), she asked us to share a brief memory. I shared this:

I was looking for a .jpeg picture the other day. I've saved all of Cooper's pictures in my iPhotos, and I have his little meme pictures from saving his data from Snapchat. It was kind of funny looking at the memes Cooper was sending to his friends in high school. He had a pretty good sense of humor. Many of the memes are totally inappropriate, and most people would not find humor in some of them, but they made me smile. The kind of things these kids sent back and forth to each other was comical. Digital natives. As Cooper got older, he was trying to wean himself off social media, and I think he was largely successful. Good on him.

At our most recent The Compassionate Friends meeting, a bereaved mom said to our group that she feels like, since her son's death, she is just drifting. I completely understand; I feel like this now. I used to believe I was an "operator," that I could influence my environment and make things happen. Now, I am in a boat drifting along parallel to the shore, waving at all the good people. Just drifting, no paddles. Waving, with a smile on my face.

I'm no longer forcing life, asserting my will. I am taking paths of less resistance, moving with the spirits. There is a flow to life; I sense it now.

Oddly, this lack of strain, this letting go, is not so bad. I am finding a new happiness in release—probably because I am now realizing how little control I actually had over anything.

Through Cooper's death, I have let go of my driven self. I am more attuned to the compassionate person within me that I have always been but have not let out because of life and risk. It's risky to be authentically ourselves and show that to other people. But now, to heck with it.

My kids are doing well, all things considered. I am anchored at the reef, wrecked, and doing my part to full-send them into the world. Mama Bear and I have each other. We are doing spiritual edgework together. I've got the grief. I will hold it for all of us. Kids, you go.

A question I used to ask my children was this: "How are you... deep in your soul?" The reason for the question was because if I asked them, "How are you doing?" like we all do all the time, they would respond with "fine" or "good." So I changed the question. "How are you doing in your soul?" This caused them to pause and reflect.

How am I doing in my soul? I hurt. More on some days than others. I understand my life has been tragically altered. Even when I try to fake it and use old maxims and axioms to pump myself up, I know I have been badly wounded. My wife, tenfold.

And yet, I am still standing. I still smile, and I still have joy and happiness in my heart. I still want the best out of this life.

It's difficult for me to have conversations with people who act like they know what's up because they've gone through some stuff and all, but they have not lost a child. There's just nobody who knows except the people who know. I just can't explain this. So my peace and my love go out to those who have lost a child, who know this deep hurt place. Only they really know. When it comes to understanding the new spirit world that opens up after the loss of a child and the difficulty in straining through traditional Christian language to find words and symbols that help the grieving soul, only bereaved parents know.

I am tending, in this regard, toward more silence in my life, less noise, and fewer distractions.

As I close out my free write today, I'll share a story about Cooper that makes me smile.

From a young age, Cooper was clearly on a path toward diabetes. I jest, but the boy loved sugar, and in particular, powdered sugar. He would toast bread and use a spoon to scoop and then smooth a 1/4-inch layer of powdered sugar on each of two slices of bread, edge to edge, times two. He would then sit at the kitchen table, watching SpongeBob on the television across the room, smiling with contentment at the pure joy of sugar and SpongeBob.

One day, I took out the powdered sugar bag to make Cooper some powdered sugar toast. I felt a spoon in the bag, so I went to take it out. I noticed another spoon in the bag. Then another, and another, and another. I took five spoons out of the powdered sugar bag. Apparently, once Cooper made his toast, he simply left the spoon in the bag and moved on with his day.

These were the kinds of funny nuances of living with a gifted child. Bright, but lacking in the common sense department.

These little stories of Cooper still make me smile.

spread cooper kindness

August 23, 2024
By Nanny Kathy, Coop's grandmother

When I think of my grandson, I will always remember his character. His kind heart was genuine and compassionate; he was warm, gentle, and caring. He loved his family and his dogs. I hope his legacy will always be to spread kindness.

I still struggle with the word "suicide," as my mind still can't imagine that my grandson would take his own life.

We lived fairly close during Cooper's childhood, so we were very fortunate to share many great family holidays together. Christmas, Thanksgiving, Easter, Independence Day, and birthday celebrations were all great fun.

Cooper enjoyed barbecuing with his grandfather, otherwise known as Poppy. It was always a joy to have Cooper in our home.

During Cooper's childhood, he came for many sleepovers and also lived with us for a few months during the COVID-19 pandemic and again after his college graduation. As his "Nanny," Cooper always put a smile in my heart and a twinkle in my eye; he was indeed very special.

I often ask myself, how could I, as a grandparent, outlive my grandson?

Nanny Kathy and Cooper

My own sadness doesn't begin to touch what my son Kelly and his wife Victoria have been through this past year. As the mother of Cooper's father and Victoria's mother-in-law, I grieve that I can't fix their pain as they suffer from this enormous tragedy. Their sadness is so deep I worry for their health, knowing that grief affects the mind, body, and spirit.

I often wonder how this happened to such a precious family who loved their son so much.

I'm close to my two adult sons, and I feel very proud of how they've grown even closer through this horrific loss. In the first few days after Cooper's death, they shared heartache and horror that only a brother's bond could survive.

Those were scary and horrific days in the immediate aftermath of Cooper's death—too painful to try to share.

Cooper's Uncle Jason arrived on the first day of the impact of our loss, and he held his brother tight during his darkest hours. For several months after our loss, Kelly and I would talk and cry daily on the phone, just leaning on each other's pain.

Cooper was so loving and caring.

We believe Cooper suffered from a mental health crisis that had been lingering over the past few years, undiagnosed. Cooper had a few counseling sessions in recent years, but we never understood the depth of his pain.

Yes, this is what we mostly say to outsiders, but honestly, we just don't have any other answers. We just don't know. We are left wondering, how could we not know Cooper's pain was so deep, and that he was able to hide it so well?

On the outside looking in, things looked amazing. Cooper had recently graduated from college with a degree in Aerospace Engineering, he had a good job at the university, a new car, and a solid bank account. But still, his world was crushing him with loneliness, depression, and a lack of self-worth that finally tormented him to end his own precious life.

Our family is devastated and broken.

My son and his family will always have that missing piece of their son and brother. We will forever mourn Cooper, the loss of his future, and the promise of the dreams that lay ahead of him.

Cooper was loved, and he loved his family. He was not heavily into alcohol or drugs; he took good care of his body. During his time living with us, I would be in awe of him swimming 100 laps, playing golf, taking hour-long runs through the neighborhood, working out in the village gym, and eating a healthy diet.

Cooper James: 23 years old.

How could there be such a short END date for such an extraordinary young man?

On the day of Cooper's burial, October 20th, 2023, my son officiated the burial of his son.

There are no words to describe the heartfelt spiritual presence that took place on that day.

Only by the grace of God was Kelly able to stand before his family and give Cooper back to God.

I witnessed the Holy Spirit take Cooper's soul into His heavenly kingdom during his burial. The sky was blue, white birds flew above, and a shiny perpetual light flowed through the tall trees. Go home, our son, it is your time to be with our Lord.

We were so blessed to have you in our lives for 23 short years, Cooper.

Years ago, I gave Cooper a prayer candle and a rosary. Cooper kept these on his dresser. In pictures, he often wore a patron saint necklace. Cooper was baptized and confirmed in the Roman Catholic Church.

I put the rosary from his dresser in his hands and buried it with him in his casket.

The Lord took Cooper home. I was there, this I do know.

I think I've learned that the grief of Cooper's death is a pain we will sit with now and always, never having the answers as to why he took his own life.

Now we must learn to remember how beautiful our love for him was and is, and to hold tight to the memories we cherish.

Victoria was everything a mother could be. I remember her working tediously over the years, making photo scrapbooks for each of her children, my grandchildren. Now, Cooper's scrapbooks are a family treasure; we value Victoria's work that captures each year of his childhood through high school graduation.

We all have special memories of what a wonderful, precious life Cooper lived, and we know not to take this fragile, wondrous life for granted.

There is nothing left to fear after a family suffers a tragedy like this. Nothing. My love for my grandson lives on as I await our heavenly reunion.

I want to live out my life spreading 'Cooper Kindness' to all in honor of him.

Forever loved,

Nanny Kathy

~

i love you

August 28, 2024
By Jason, Coop's uncle

My brother, my mom, this family—we will never be the same. We will never know what Cooper was going through or why he took his own life. I wish we could go back to life before October 8th, 2023. I wish we could have prevented this. I believe if Cooper could have made it through those moments, then hours, then days, perhaps he would have found hope and gotten through his difficult time.

I visited Cooper during his senior year while he was in college. I remember telling him, "I love you." This was just a couple of years ago. Kelly had asked me to go check on Cooper in his apartment. He did not seem to be in a good way. He looked at me with skepticism when I told him, "I love you."

I said, "Watch, Cooper. There will come a day when your brothers and sister will have children, and you will love them. I don't know why or how it works, but you just do." His eyes rolled up into his head just a little as if he was imagining being an uncle. Then a small smile cracked from under the pain, and there I saw hope in his eyes. Perhaps that is what got him through the next couple of years. I know that Cooper seemed happiest when he was with his brothers.

I have a lot of memories of Cooper. They make me smile and sustain me.

The Boys

I only saw Cooper a few times each year, even though I was his godfather. My earliest memory of Cooper is from when my wife, Cooper's "Aunt Shell," and I first moved back to Arizona from Tennessee. We lived with Kelly's family for a couple of months while Cooper was a baby. I smile as I remember Victoria freaking out because I was bouncing Cooper a little too roughly in his bouncer. What did I know about babies?

For many years, our families gathered together in Southern Arizona for the 4th of July. I remember playing football with all the boys. Cooper could get considerably competitive. He showed no let-up for his younger cousin, Ry.

When Kelly and Victoria moved to Montana, my family flew out to go skiing. This was just before the pandemic. On our drive to Red Lodge ski resort, I remember Cooper and Carse bitching and arguing with each other over how far away a mountain was. Cooper said, "Carse is acting like a little bitch." It cracked me up because Cooper was the younger brother, and he was holding his brother to account, standing up to him.

Cooper was a rule follower, mostly, especially when the rules came from his mom. I remember Cooper refused to eat chips in the living room on the carpet because his mom had made the rule not to. I gave him permission, and Victoria was not there, but Cooper still wouldn't do it.

I remember yelling at Cooper once while we were playing. The look he gave me made me realize to never make that mistake again. I hurt his feelings. Cooper was a sensitive soul.

Cooper was a great cousin to my son, Ry. They spent a couple of days at the ski resort shredding together. They were both diehard soccer fans. They'd go kick the soccer ball together at Nanny's house. They also took rides on the golf cart and did all the things cousins do—probably some things I don't know about.

I know that Cooper was hurting. When I went to check on him after Kelly asked me to, I knew he wasn't doing well. I told Kelly he should come get him, and he did. Kelly flew out to Arizona, picked up his boy, and drove back home with him. With Cooper being at home with his mom and dad, landing a job, he appeared to get his life together after several years of hard work. He was doing well.

There's so much pain and tragedy in the world, but until October 8th, 2023, it had never touched our family so profoundly. Those stories you see on television—the awful, tragic things most people never imagine—have touched our family, and we will never be the same. It has forever changed us.

Our family is broken into two pieces. There is the family before October 8th, when we were living it up, and now there is the family after October 8th, where it will never be the same.

BUT, we can still find laughter, genuine laughter, and spaces without thought, spaces without shadows, and joy, love, and hope. Especially hope.

We miss you, Cooper James, and just like I told you at the University of Arizona, I love you. I will always remember you.

Cooper had a tragic accident as a result of mental illness or depression. This does not define the beautiful young man he was. In my mind, what happened to Cooper is no different than cancer. Cooper got sick, and like a collapsing star, he imploded.

I don't know why I love you, Cooper, but I just do. Just like I do all my nieces and nephews.

My godson. Dang. Something got messed up and went wrong. How did this happen? Rest in peace, Cooper.

Love,

Uncle Jason

~

surfers, mosaic artists, and carpenters
September 8, 2024

During the summer of 2018, I spent four months working on our house in Southern Arizona, preparing to sell it. We were moving to Montana. It was a fine summer, one of my favorites. I worked with my hands, used a variety of tools, and connected in a deep way with the objective reality of rehabbing our house.

When I swung my hammer, I hit the nail solid, or I didn't. The world was real, and it did not lie.

I was living my best life. While I was not technically a "professor," this fact did not hinder my students from calling me one. I was working at the university in the mountains, teaching in the fire science program and running it. Because I was on an academic schedule, I had four months off. I was home on summer break, preparing our house to sell, before our final move up north.

As I prepped our house for the market, I tiled our master bathroom. I used a beautiful porcelain 36" tile with ridges and contours. I set the tile on a diagonal, and it looked sharp. It lit the master bathroom up. It was a nice upgrade.

The water in Arizona is hard, loaded with minerals and quick to stain and leave deposits on glass shower doors. I tried, at first, to scrub the existing shower doors clean but quickly realized the best move was to buy new doors.

I was home alone. The new doors were purchased and in the garage. I took one of the old glass doors off, out of the rails, and was carefully walking it out of the bathroom. One of the corners hit the new tile floor, and the glass door instantly disintegrated in my hands. It literally turned to dust, shattering into a trillion pieces. I stood there in disbelief, holding my breath so as not to inhale the fine glass shards.

It took me the rest of the day to clean up the glass. I imagine there are still little pieces of glass in that bathroom somewhere.

This immediate shattering, a disintegration into a trillion pieces, is what happened to our lives 11 months ago, on October 8th, when we learned Cooper was gone, by his own volition.

Instant. Dust.

I have had hard times in life. No surprise, we all have. If you're a Christian, you know you will bear a cross at some point in time. If you're a Buddhist, you know life is suffering. If you're an atheist, sometimes life is just a flat-out suck fest. The journey is sometimes rough, the valleys often unforgiving, and, god dammit Mama, you never told me there would be days like this.

But like a reed in the wind, when I have experienced pain and suffering in the past—the valley lows, those unforgiving life circumstances—I bent far over, but I never broke. Until now.

I think, retrospectively, lacking humility, breathing big and puffing up with hubris, I fancied myself as something special. I bent far over, touched the ground, cried, hurt, felt pain, but somehow regained my shape and became a reed reaching for the sun again, no longer bent over, touching the ground.

Fall down seven, rise eight.

Then, Cooper. Shattered. There is no regaining my previous shape. A threshold was reached, and I broke. I am broken. A trillion pieces of Dad, lying on the bathroom floor.

Not just my body, but the inside, too. My soul. My heart, my will, my spirit.

Let's be honest, a good mosaic artist can't put a trillion pieces back together again. Even if it were possible—damn, that's an interesting human. That's not a human.

So it's transformation then, a reorganization into a new person —a new husband, dad, son, brother, friend, coworker.

This is why we say there is a cost to resilience. Scars. Shadows. Crossing thresholds, transformation, reorganization into something new.

As I reorganize, I find my confidence as a parent has been shaken. Again, in hubris, I once believed myself a pretty darned good father. I felt like we, as parents, fairly well had our shit together. We did all the things good parents do. Nice homes, good neighborhoods, quality education, solid friends, time together as a family, dinner together, sports, church, family vacations, music, art, an active interest in our children's lives, love, care, tenderness, and toughness, too. Lions must roll. And so we did.

I took pride in the fact that we never used child care while our kids were growing up. We made choices. It was just us, mom and dad, raising our children together. As a firefighter, I would get off shift in the morning, go home, and put my kids in a baby backpack and go for a hike, or a baby stroller and go run. I cherished our afternoon naps together.

We were able to get all three of our sons through college debt-free, and we will do the same for our daughter, who is now in college. I used to admire this accomplishment.

As I consider my children today, and what I have to offer them, I am thankful they are older. I am skittish to offer them advice, to say too much, to lean in too far. I fear—did I lean in too much in Cooper's life? Was I overbearing? Did my advice hurt more than help? Or, was I not there enough, too absent?

What role did I have in my son's demise? It can't be that it takes a village to raise a child, but when they take their own lives, they are on their own, 100% responsible.

About two years ago, I sat in a restaurant and watched young children running and screaming through the aisles while their parents sat back and said nothing. They thought it was cute. These "parents" acted like their children's best friends, not parents. I remember thinking to myself, "what a shit show." Now, I pause. I pause some more, and I think, what the fuck do I know? Actually, probably not much. You know what, screw it —run kids, run! Jump on the tables, bounce from booth to booth, show your best friends what you're capable of.

As a parent, then, on the backside of losing a child, I find my confidence in fathering shaken. I wonder, would I come to me for parental advice? I don't know.

We—my wife, our children, and I—have gone through a lot these past 11 months. We have experienced many firsts. Immediately, in October, we celebrated two birthdays without Cooper. Then Thanksgiving, Christmas, New Year's, Mother's Day, Father's Day, Cooper's Birthday, Fourth of July, and family vacations, all without Cooper.

Each of those days was hard. I am experiencing renewed sadness and grief as we approach October 8th, the one-year anniversary of Cooper's death. As the seasons change, the cool mornings set in, the leaves change color and begin to fall, and school starts, there are several familiar signs that have me feeling it in the body.

It's true, what they say—the body does keep the score. The issues are in the tissues.

Meaning, the mind/brain is connected through a thousand-billion neural pathways to the body, the gut, the heart, the belly, etc. Our mind is literally in the body. All of the reminders, the pain, and the grief that shattered me on October 8th—my body knows this date is coming up again, and it's guarding up.

The good news is, I recognize it. I know my body keeps the score, and I know I have many issues in my tissues that are going to flex during this next month. I see you, body. I certainly feel you.

Metacognition. I see myself thinking about the issues in my tissues. Meta-emoting. I feel myself feeling the feelings.

The obstacle is the way, right? The only way out is through, right? When you think you're done, you're only 40% done, right?

Check in on myself. Breathe. Ground.

Chin up, shoulders back. Stand tall. Be strong and courageous. Never, never, never give up.

And so it goes, daily.

I've always been a little strange. My firefighter buddies used to bust my chops and tell me I would drive a convertible MG and ride around with a tweed coat and skull cap and be a professor. They were not far off.

But I do find myself even a bit stranger these days. I notice small things, especially animals and nature. I am very attuned to nature these days, and especially birds. I am captivated by birds. Or are they souls stopping by to say, "hi?" And which one of you is Cooper?

Before this tragedy unfolded in our lives, I was learning Finnish. It's quite an interesting language. It's a Uralic language, and not something we are used to hearing. Our ears are attuned to Romance languages, but not Uralic.

Learning a new language is challenging; we all know this. The best way to learn a new language is immersion. Here I am, right here, right now. I am learning the new language of grief.

Part of this new language is learning to speak with nature and birds and red foxes. Most bereaved parents and siblings already know this grief language. You learn it quickly. It's like we're all deaf, signing to each other, and having a conversation about spirits and birds and souls and issues in the tissues and all of the things, and nobody else knows what we are saying.

11 months. Damn.

I rarely watch television. Lately, I have been watching the documentary, *100 Foot Wave*.[1] I am watching it over and over and over again. I love it.

Why am I drawn to the ocean and waves in this season of my life, as I am reorganizing myself, transforming, on the other side of crossing a threshold? Why is the laid-back surfing life speaking to my soul so strongly? Why does Nazaré, Portugal present to me as so appealing while watching this documentary?

Perhaps, I wonder, if I could go back and do it all over again, and if our family were a laid-back surfing family, would it have made all the difference?

If Cooper were raised as a surfer, would I be writing this blog post right now?

Victoria and I started off doing it right. We did. Then we got caught in the hype, living the American dream. Working hard, earning the money, paying the bills, focusing on the kids, wanting to give them the best life.

And, perhaps, all they ever wanted to be were surfers, mosaic artists, and carpenters, swinging a hammer true.

Such is the new language of grief...

Dad and Coop

theological three sisters

H ere we are. October 8th, the one-year anniversary of Cooper's death, is two weeks away. This has been a year in the dark wilderness, for sure.

In these last few weeks leading up to this significant mile maker in our lives, I have certainly felt it in my mind, body, and soul. Deep in my bones. The grief has come pouring back down, big wave sets, crashing over me. A new first, the anniversary of Cooper's death, and more freezing.

I believe, the body does keep the score, the issues are in the tissues, and what fires together, wires together. I don't even have to be conscious of it, my body just knows and it tells my mind, *hey, things are not okay, I remember this date.*

The cooling of the weather, the back-to-school routines, the leaves falling from the trees, the college kids back in town— *yeah, this all spells trouble.* Or so my body would have my mind believe.

All the biological, neurological things are happening. Through a trillion neurological connections, I am experiencing it.

After a year of navigating grief, the ground truth remains: I miss my son. I loved him so much. I still love him so much. I long for him to be here again.

Melancholy Man, big gaping hole right through center mass. Double-tapped.

I know Cooper will not be here in this life again, and this is so painful to accept. I will have to continue to navigate my life on this earth without him until it's my time to put my angel wings on.

When I see my boy again, we are going to do a little tap dog dance on the pinheads. An angelic Irish celebration, or Australian Tap Dog hustle.

You've heard me say this before, and you have read it in my writing: I am 100% confident I will see my son again. This is truth. I have confidence I will be with all of my family *del otro lado*.

I can't explain this to you; I just know it.

I have always shared with my children that there are three main questions we have to grapple with and come to terms with in this life. These questions, the Theological Three Sisters, are:

1. Where did we come from?
2. Why are we here?
3. Where are we going after death?

The answers to these questions, maybe even the grappling with them to figure them out, tell us a lot about a person. It's defining. It shapes our life. Even not grappling with these questions says something.

While I have spent the last year navigating grief, striving to keep my nose above the waterline, I have also been spiritually grappling with the Theological Three Sisters' existential questions.

Where did Cooper go? What is he doing now? And what will it be like when I see him again?

As I have wrestled with more existential questions, I have needed time and space. As such, I have been disinclined to attend traditional church and to be preached at/to. I don't have the ears for it in this season of life.

Shall we draw theological swords and wax sanctification, justification, glorification, predestination, cosmology, eschatology, and dominion theology?

I'm out. Do your thing. I yield.

I have found a beautiful new spiritual home in a small, nonprogrammed Friends church. You know, the Quakers. The Meeting provides me with the spiritual space I need in this season of life to process, form, and continue my spiritual growth in a broadening-out cone. I think this small foundational piece of my life would be honoring to Cooper. Cooper loved silence and stillness. This is the essence of Quaker worship.

For me, I have accepted that silence is a new sacrament in my life.

Two roads diverged in a wood, and I—

I continue to be grateful for my wife, my daughter, my sons, my brother, my parents, my mother-in-law, my dogs, my Friends community, my family and friends, my health, and the fact that I am still smiling, standing, and breathing, even though I hurt badly.

Family, friends, as we come to pass this one year anniversary of

Cooper's death in two weeks, my intention is to step away from writing on this blog. It's time for me to wrap it up.

I finally went back and read through all of my blog posts, and I believe I have written everything I have to say.

For the last year, I have laid myself bare for the whole world to see, and I have been vulnerable in a very public space.

Why have I done this?

I have shared deeply from my heart because I don't want any more young men and women to take their own lives. I don't want anyone of any age to take their own life, but especially young men and women.

I don't want moms and dads, brothers and sisters, family and friends, communities, to have to experience this. It's terrible; it really is.

Further, if someone will experience the loss of a child or a sibling in the future, or has more recently experienced the loss of a child or sibling, I have been hopeful my words would be helpful. I wanted to let others know they are not alone, that we understand, and that you are going to make it—but the road is tough.

People do get beat up in the dark wilderness. This is for real.

I have also been hopeful that as a man who has spent a career in a high-risk operational environment (fire service), I would be able to provide some space for grown men to grieve openly, to see that it is okay to roll with lions and grieve. Both are okay.

I have been hopeful that in some small way, my writing has helped the human condition. I am showing up, and you are hearing my voice.

I have often shared with my children, *"the Creation waits in eager expectation for the sons and daughters of God to reveal themselves."*

I am revealing myself. You see me.

There are two things I want you to know.

Cooper's memorial stone, as viewed from the backside

First, Cooper's Memorial Stone is mounted at the cemetery. It is beautiful. The granite stone is from South Dakota and is called Blue Bahama. When I learned about this stone, I knew immediately this was the stone for his memorial. We are really happy with the simple yet unique shape of this stone. I think we did good. I understand the workers who installed the stone were impressed with our design.

Secondly, I/we are doing okay. We really are. We are going to make it. Our grief is stabilized, we are functioning reasonably well, and we are reasonably happy inside and out.

We're broken, yes. But our love for Cooper will always be there, and it's not going away. We will love and honor our boy moving forward in life the best we can. There will be ups and downs; we will hurt, we will continue to grieve, and we will continue to go on casting our shadows about. And yet, we will do our best to be grateful in this life, for our children, our pets, and for what we do have.

Third, there is another blog post coming, and this last blog post will be from my wife, Victoria. She will close things out, as it were.

I believe Mom should have the last word.

In closing, while this list is not exhaustive, this is what I have learned over the last year.

- If you lose a child or sibling or grandchild or good friend, your soul is going to ache like nothing you have ever experienced before. This is going to hurt so bad. I am sorry.
- Successful, loved people can and will take their own lives. I never thought this would happen to us; it was not even on my mind. And yet, here we are. There were over 50,000 suicides in 2023, and over 100,000 drug overdoses. Why? We should be talking about this.
- The loss of a loved one, like a grandpa, may be a trigger for those suffering with mental health issues, e.g., depression. A string of triggers may be harmful.
- We need to end the stigma surrounding mental health issues. There is no shame in having mental health situations arise, and if you need to go pro, go pro.

Depression is a global pandemic, and the rates of depression in the US are the highest they have ever been. Fact.

- If you can see your loved one before they are buried or cremated, go see them. It made a big, positive difference for us.
- Anoint your child with oils.
- I hope you have a community that will surround you and help you during the toughest months of your life.
- The cards, the doorbell ringing, the flowers, the food, will quickly end. Supporters have a limited attention span.
- In the early days, especially, keep talking with close family and friends. You have to talk it out. Keep talking.
- People will grieve in different ways, and at different paces. There's no right way to grieve, but we do have an obligation to grieve in a healthy manner. Society (family and friends) will want you to get over your grief quickly.
- This grief will be with you the rest of your life. You learn to cope with it; your strength grows in parallel with your grief.
- You will talk in circles, there will be way more questions than answers, and you will end up at the same dead-end in many conversations. Nonetheless, keep talking.
- Don't be afraid to take a road trip when the dust settles a little bit. Get on the road and just breathe.
- Create an altar. Light candles (use battery-operated candles that look real; we have one lit 24x7).
- You will have trouble thinking and remembering for many months.
- You will deal with complex emotions you have never dealt with before. This emotional landscape, this traumascape, is tough.

- Stand together with family and friends. Put your feet underneath your shoulders and stand tall; get grounded.
- Anchor in, be prepared for spiritual edgework.
- Breathe. Ground. Pray.
- Rugged hope is more important than resilience. You are not going to bounce back.
- This loss will impact many people. The butterfly effect. Spiritual ripples.
- Lie to yourself and say, "The best days of my life are ahead of me." Repeat it over and over again.
- You will grieve for the future—what you will have missed, what will never happen.
- This loss will affect every aspect of your life—your mind, body, spirit, social life, and work life.
- Writing may help. It helped me.
- Routine is important.
- Holidays are very, very difficult. The emotions will come up. This first anniversary of Cooper's death, damn.
- You are never going to be healed, but healing will take place.
- It will be hard to breathe and stand in the early days. You won't know what day it is.
- It will be hard to trust life again. If this can happen, then all bets are off; anything can happen. This is how it feels.
- People you least expect will come out of the woodwork to help you. And others you would expect the most from will fall flat.
- Grief comes in wave sets.
- You may freeze.
- Water, hiking, nature, and animals are healing.
- Music, art, poetry, and nature may speak the "words" you need to hear more than your religious tradition.
- You may experience a faith shift. You may lose your faith.

- You may talk to the dead. This is okay. You will pray more for and to the dead than you ever did.
- Animals, insects, and sounds (wind chimes, crows) take on new meaning.
- You may "see" spirits everywhere. You will be super close to thin spaces.
- Depression is not going to show up in a young man like society has depicted it. They may not lay in bed all day and mope. Cooper did not.
- Emotions get mixed up. Even happy, good emotions get mixed up with grief.
- Your system can get overstimulated much easier. Too many people, too much noise, too much movement. Stay away from these in the early days.
- You will not forget your child, your brother, your grandchild, your friend. This was my earliest fear. I now have confidence: I will never forget my son.
- You are never going to be the same. A demarcation line has been drawn. There was life before this loss, and now life after. You are a different person. Transformation.
- Don't be afraid to experiment with new altars and sacraments in your life, whatever that may mean to you.
- You will now notice the small things—a ladybug on a flower is an entire universe. You will stop and consider them, both the flower and ladybug.
- You will be more compassionate toward others. You will move slower and listen more deeply.
- You will speak a special language now that only other bereaved parents and siblings will understand.

And on and on the list will go. These are the quick things that come to my mind.

Friends, I love you.

From the deep place where the coins are, thank you for picking them up with me over this last year.

Blessings,

Kelly

∼

just to be with you

October 8, 2024

By Victoria, Coop's mom

Dear Cooper,

I miss you. It is impossible to explain how broken my heart is without you here. I am so, so sorry that I did not understand what was going on. Moms are supposed to know these things. I look at your pictures in disbelief every day. The pain of never seeing you again, and how you must have felt that night, is just incomprehensible to my brain. I talk to you in my mind a lot. I pretend I see you standing outside the front door by the wind chimes that were sent for you. And I hope every day that if I pray hard enough, if I will it hard enough, if I am nice enough, somehow you will come back. My brain and heart just can't function knowing that you are gone. I doubt they ever will—the hole, the crack, is just too big.

I wish you could have seen yourself through everyone else's eyes, Coopie. Everyone knew what a sweetheart you were with those big eyes and kind disposition. You were "famous" from an early age, as the "baby in the backpack" at all the soccer games that Dad and I coached for CJ. You were quite well known throughout the soccer community and helped coach from the backpack as we coached CJ's and then Carse's soccer teams. It was no surprise that you were an excellent soccer player from the start of your soccer debut at five years old, and that was the sport you truly loved and played through college.

You were talking at an early age and started so many sentences when you were two years old with, "Actually…" You loved going to the "movieator" and having "mintens" at Abuelo's. When you started first grade, the teacher wanted to have you tested for the gifted program. Dad and I weren't sure that was a good idea, since Carse and CJ were already in it, and we didn't want you to feel any pressure.

Coop and Mom

So we just told you that you were going to do some fun activities with a teacher. But you literally aced those three tests with a 99, a 99++, and another 99++. I had to ask the gifted teacher what this even meant, and she told me to get you in any activity that you wanted to do. You were off the charts smart, literally, and got the nickname "Baby Einstein."

You held yourself to such high academic standards—you absolutely hated busy work in class and always wanted a challenge to learn more. You announced during testing one year that you were reading the dictionary while the class had to be quiet until everyone was done testing. You loved talking in different language accents and even convinced Grace that you were one of Santa's elves because of how much you loved powdered sugar.

And then there was the "pickle" phase that never really ended—always telling everyone that they were a pickle, or including it however you could fit it in. I about had a heart attack when you wanted to build your own computer for your ninth-grade birthday, but that was silly of me, because like everything else, it was perfect. You graduated sixth in your class out of 400 kids and, of course, chose Aerospace Engineering for your major.

Engineering had definitely been on your mind for years, because you were always building things. We would be at Starbucks, and you were making a tower with their bananas by the cash register. We went to the diner while visiting Nanny and Poppy, and you made a tower of the coffee creamers. You would take all of the silverware at a table and try to stack them. You stayed home sick one day in high school, and I came home to a tower of Tupperware when you were feeling better and got bored. You even stacked all of the Rummikub tiles at Thanksgiving 2021, and we bet a tequila shot. Yes, remember—I lost, and I had the shot.

Mom and Cooper

Your kind, quiet demeanor attracted the best of friends— Buckley in preschool, Colton in kindergarten, and then you met Ethan in first grade. We kept hearing all about Ethan every day, although we had not met him yet. And you two even got in trouble once or twice for being silly in class. We finally met Ethan at his birthday party in December that year, and you were fast friends—in class together, played soccer together, graduated high school together, and were roommates your freshman year in college. Jonathan, Jacob, Cash, and Austin were also great friends through high school and college. You had a group of friends, and you all had so much in common, and they all could care less that you were the quiet one.

Then you met Chase at college in your fraternity and had another incredible friend. So even though you thought you needed to be more chatty and social, the best of friends were still finding you.

The funny thing is, Coopie, anyone who was around you knew that you could get quite crazy. Do you remember the 7:30 pm Cooper time when you just seemed to get wound up like crazy every night? Your second-grade sleepover for your birthday, where you didn't even go to sleep? How crazy you were on the sixth-grade California field trip when your teacher said she laughed at this side of you that she had never seen at school? But you were obviously being an incredibly kind person to everyone all of the time, because I remember a mom calling in fifth grade to invite you to her daughter's birthday party. I had never heard the little girl's name before and asked you about her. You told me that she didn't have many friends, but you just always tried to be nice to her. You were clearly doing a stellar job of being kind and including her.

Dad and I were so excited when you took the job at the university when you graduated. It was always so hard not having you, Carse, or CJ here, and the fact that we had you here made everything so much better. We were obviously misled by your busyness, as I am guessing you did that to keep your brain occupied, much like I do now to be able to handle the pain. You were working, going to the gym, teaching yourself how to play the guitar, golfing, relearning French, taking flight lessons to get your pilot's license, and hanging out with Abby and her friends.

It always made me laugh that it took Amy and me so long to get you and Abby connected as friends, but once again, Abby was a gem of a friend and misses you so much too. The year we had you here was just perfect. I even told you how much I had missed you when you were only gone five days on your trip to Florida in September. You said you had really missed me too. I loved seeing you every day, and it was crazy how hard those five days were with you gone. But then less than three weeks later, I couldn't even fathom how I would go on without you here. I still don't know. I go through the motions like everyone else. I know you understood how much we all loved you, but it wasn't enough.

Snoopy follows Dad around most of the time these days. You sure were good at picking out "Rowdy" to join our family. When we come in from pottying, he stops underneath your wind chimes and looks intently at the space. That's why I think you are there somewhere—I think Snoopy knows. When CJ and Carse come, Snoopy tends to want to go out in the front yard looking for you. He about broke my heart even more at Christmas because he wanted to be out front so much. He knows you should be here, and he kept looking.

Coopie, I know you know that our family of six is everything to me. I know you knew that. That's why I know you had to be in so much pain, because I know you knew that you being gone would figuratively "kill" me. I do still love teaching—I think I am pretty good at it—but my brain has to compartmentalize each day so that I can try and give my best in the classroom. I have several teacher friends who have lost sons. They understand. One of them says her brain has to have different rooms, so that she can cope with things. I thought it was a good analogy. I have to close your door at school if I can, so that I can function for the children. The door is usually wide open on the way to school, though, and also as soon as I walk out of school. I cry in the car a lot. The door also cracks open at school, and I just do the best I can. I have your picture in a frame by itself so that I can look at you during the day. I was afraid it would make me cry, since I do that most of the time when I look at your pictures. But instead, it makes me feel like you are there watching me. I bought a bracelet with a little tiny "C" on it. My fingers rub the "C" a lot as I think about you.

Mom and Cooper

As we come up on the one year anniversary of enduring life without you, I wanted to think of some of the happy memories I have of you. I know there are plenty of people that would be happy to listen to me talk about you, but it's hard. It is all hard. I still can't talk about you without crying.

While I know we weren't the best singers when you were in eighth grade, we would sing One Direction's "What Makes You Beautiful" in the car on the way to soccer practice and games. I still sing it like you are there with me when it comes up on my playlist.

I think Aunt Krissie or Cousin Kristi sent me a song from Scott Calum, *You Are the Reason*.[1] It wasn't written for a mom losing a child, but I play it a lot in the car, listen to it, and cry. The phrases in the song say it so well.

I would, I'd give anything just to be with you again.

I love you, Coopie.

Love,

Mom

~

honoring cooper

T his has been the toughest year of my (our) life. Period.

I would, however, like to end on a positive note, with my head up, shoulders back, eyes to the heavens, and showing my face to Creation.

I intend to honor Cooper with my life, and this book is at least a start in that direction.

It's important for me to share with you a few ways, I think, that would be honoring to Cooper.

Embrace the Quiet

Cooper found joy in the simple, quiet moments of life. For example, he enjoyed playing and practicing soccer with his friends, or by himself, quietly kicking the ball around the pitch. He enjoyed working out at the gym and in the garage hitting the heavy bag. Cooper loved spending time with family and friends watching television or just being with his dog, Snoopy.

Whether it's a small garden, a quiet corner in the house, or a spot under a favorite tree, create a space where you can go to remember Cooper or your loved one in quiet. Find a place that reflects the calm and peace Cooper sought, where you can feel close to him. All the better if the place has wind chimes and animals scurrying about.

I used to watch Cooper sit on the back porch and eat a meal in silence, quietly taking in the birds, the squirrels, the sun, and the wind.

Set your phone and screens down, turn your face toward the sun, lean your head back, close your eyes, and take a slow, deep breath. Smile. Where are you? You're right here, right now.

Honoring Cooper could mean taking time to find peace in the quiet.

Celebrate Cooper's Passions

Engage with the things Cooper loved (or things you love) to do. For example, play soccer, watch *The Office*, learn French, complete a 500-piece puzzle, play the guitar, play golf, play *League of Legends*, spend time outdoors flying a drone, or get outside and enjoy nature.

Cooper enjoyed taking the dogs for walks at the lake and conservation area. He had an inflatable tube in the trunk of his car for chilling on the lake.

Cooper has several nature pictures saved in his files. He noticed nature, and this is something I wasn't aware of before his death.

Continue Cooper's Curiosity

Cooper was always curious, always learning. Take up a new hobby, read a book (he never finished *Dune*, hint, hint...), or explore a topic that interests you. These small acts of nurturing your curiosity could be a way to carry forward Cooper's love for learning and discovery. I am still wondering about the silver coins Cooper was setting on the fenceposts for the crows in the backyard. This is a curious thing I aim to spend a little time with, discovering what Cooper was up to.

I also know Cooper was planning to build a chicken coop in the backyard. He had a curiosity about this.

Support Others in Struggle

We strongly believe that Cooper would want you to reach out and support those who are struggling with mental health issues or feeling lonely and isolated. Remember, Cooper loved his family and friends fiercely. Raising awareness, advocating for better support systems (especially at the university), or just being there for someone in need would honor the compassionate side of Cooper. Together, in honor of Cooper, let's help end the stigma surrounding mental health, especially in young men.

Keep Cooper's Memory Alive

If you knew Cooper, talk about him, please. Share his stories, his witty sense of humor, and the unique things he did that made him who he was. Create routines and spaces to share these memories, keeping Cooper's spirit alive in your heart.

Incidentally, I love hearing Cooper stories. If you have some good ones, please, do tell.

Be Kind and Gentle

Cooper had a kind, gentle, and caring nature. He really did. Continue this legacy by being kind to yourself and others, especially in difficult times. Compassion, patience, and understanding were a big part of who Cooper was.

Honor Cooper's Love for Animals

Cooper loved dogs and hedgehogs. In truth, he was an all-around animal lover. Continue Cooper's advocacy for animal welfare by supporting your local humane society, adopting a pet in his memory, or volunteering time or resources to causes that help animals in need.

Live Authentically

Honor Cooper by living your own life as true to yourself as possible. Be open to exploring your thoughts and feelings, and give yourself permission to be who you are, without judgment. Smile, and don't be too hard on yourself. Especially, don't apply rigid perfectionism to yourself.

If you want to go to Norway and live near the water, then find a friend and go. Cooper talked about playing soccer in Europe when he was in high school—maybe he should have done that. He also talked about moving to the Caribbean with a friend—maybe he should have done that too.

Stay Connected

Lastly, we know that Cooper valued his relationships deeply. Cooper had a few deep friendships that lasted years. Make it a point to stay connected with family and friends, support each other, and nurture the bonds that bind us. Be tribe.

Ultimately, we believe Cooper would want all of us to find healing and peace in whatever way feels right.

By taking the time and being intentional in honoring Cooper, he will always be a part of us. He will live within our hearts and our souls.

Cooper will endure because our love for him endures.

#LA FIN

acknowledgments

In writing this book, I owe a special thank you to my high school English teacher, Ms. Sabrack, for believing in me and my writing. Without her words of encouragement, I don't think this book would have been written.

I owe a special thank you to resilience researchers Dr. Ann S. Masten, University of Minnesota, and Dr. Michael Ungar, Resilience Research Center, Dalhousie University, whose work has informed my understanding of resilience, and without which, I don't know if I would be doing "okay" today.

I am indebted to the fire service for my early "steeling," and learning what it takes to face adversity squarely.

I am thankful and grateful for The Compassionate Friends (TCF) organization. I am especially grateful for our local TCF chapter leader, Sarah Kelly. She was an early (and continuing) support in helping to lift our heads above the waterline. I am also thankful for our new friends at TCF who walk with us on this painful journey.

I am thankful and grateful for the "prayer warriors" in Tubac, Arizona: Valerie Lavender, Locha Pottinger, Irene Wisdom, Dhana Waken, Rosie Cornelius, and Fr. Joseph Esson.

I want to acknowledge the Quakers in my local community who have held my family in the Light over the past year and who have supported me in my spiritual growth on the backside of child loss.

A special thank you and blessing to my friend Marilyn Pilkey for praying deeply for our family, and for reading a draft of this book and helping me edit.

A special thank you and blessing for my friend Rachel S. for reading a draft of this book and her careful editing.

A special thank you and blessing for Annette Collins for reading a draft of this book and making it better. I am very appreciative.

I must thank my brother Fr. Michael Medis for carrying me in the early days of Cooper's death. He was a solid support, and I am forever grateful.

Thank you to the men and women of our local Sheriff's Office for helping to get us off to the best start possible. We appreciate you.

A special thank you to the wonderful Langston Hughes school community for their early support and lifting us up when we were on our knees.

A special thank you to Jeff S. for being my unofficial counselor in the early months of my grief.

A special thank you to Elizabeth Leon for her comfort call.

A special thank you to Jason Cauley, a friend who came out of the woodwork over the past year and checked in on me regularly to ask how I was doing. The same goes for our long-time family friend, and my second Mom, Linda Rogers.

A special thank you to Abby Weyand, Clarissa Banks, and Karen Wiley. You all are simply the best.

A heartfelt, deep bow to the friends who were close to Cooper's heart, most especially Ethan, Jacob, Johnathan, Chase, Nik, and Abby. Cooper loved you.

A special thank you to our dearest family friends, Amy and Pat Easum for being there, always.

A very special thank you to all of our family and friends for holding space for our family over the past year.

A loving tribute to my brother, Jason McCoy, and my mom, Kathy Cathey, for being there for us through it all.

Finally, I owe the happiness of my life to my wife, children, and pets. Being a husband, father, and dog dad is my *why*. Our Party of Six means the world to me and I must acknowledge the special privilege I have to be called "Dear" and "Dad." Victoria, CJ, Carse, Cooper, and Grace, I love you with all my heart. Willow, Snoopy, and Bear Bear, you, too, have my heart.

endnotes

Introduction

1. McCoy, Kelly. *Endure*. https://endure.blog. Accessed 26 Oct. 2024.

Spiritual Edgework

1. Lois, Jennifer. *Heroic Efforts: The Emotional Culture of Search and Rescue Volunteers*. NYU Press, 2003.
2. If you're interested in learning more about "edgework" and its principles, check out the episode *Edgework* from the podcast *Rescue: Defying Fate, Defining Heroes*, hosted by Donny Dust (June 14, 2023). Available on Apple Podcasts: https://podcasts.apple.com/us/podcast/edgework/id1571571313?i= 1000617213616."
3. *Red Bird Ministries*, www.redbird.love

Rugged Hope

1. Ungar, Michael. *Working with Children and Youth with Complex Needs: 2nd Edition*. Oxford University Press, 2020. Resilience Research Centre, Dalhousie University. *52 Rugged and Resourced Protective Factors*. www.resilienceresearch.org.
2. Thompson, Curt. *The Deepest Place: Suffering and the Formation of Hope*. Zondervan, 2023.

Mountains of My Mind

1. Stapleton, C. (2023). *Higher* [Album]. Mercury Nashville Records.

Just Breathe and Bruises

1. McLeary, J., & Aldous, M. (Directors). (2017). *The Work* [Film]. The Orchard.
2. Pearl Jam. (2009). *Just Breathe*. On *Backspacer* [CD]. Monkeywrench Records.
3. Capaldi, Lewis. (2019). *Bruises*. On *Divinely Uninspired to a Hellish Extent* [Streaming audio]. Vertigo Berlin, Universal Music.

Crippin

1. György, Albert. *Mélancolie*, 2012. *Wikimedia Commons*, uploaded by art_inthecity, Creative Commons Attribution 2.0 Generic license, https://commons.wikimedia.org/wiki/File:M%C3%A9lancolie_by_Albert_Gy%C3%B6rgy.jpg. Accessed 25 Sept. 2024.
2. "Media Search for 'Hooded Sorrow'." *Wikimedia Commons*, 2023, https://commons.wikimedia.org/w/index.php?search=hooded+sorrow&title=Special:MediaSearch&go=Go&type=image. Accessed 25 Sept. 2024.

Here I Am

1. Aeon Timeline 3. Timeline.App Pty. Ltd, 2023.
2. Donne, John. *Devotions upon Emergent Occasions and Death's Duel*. Vintage Books, 1999, p. 108.

Red Fox

1. Cacciatore, Joanne. *Bearing the Unbearable: Love, Loss, and the Heartbreaking Path of Grief*. Wisdom Publications, 2017.
2. Mountain Dreamer, Oriah. *The Invitation*. HarperOne, 1999.

Poundmakers

1. "Poundmakers Tribute Song to Devere Tsatoke, FSIN Powwow 2011." *YouTube*, uploaded by HIGH50CIETY, 8 Oct. 2011, https://www.youtube.com/watch?v=Ib1WC43g0Zs

Good Grief

1. Crawford, Matthew B. *Shop Class as Soulcraft: An Inquiry into the Value of Work*. Penguin Books, 2009.
2. Roe, Gary. *Shattered: Surviving the Loss of a Child*. Grief.com, https://grief.com/books-on-the-loss-of-a-child/shattered-surviving-loss-child-gary-roe/
3. "Grief in Dying Often Goes Unacknowledged." *University of Helsinki*, 11 Jan. 2018, www.helsinki.fi/en/news/culture/grief-dying-often-goes-unacknowledged. Accessed 25 Sept. 2024.

Cracked Ones

1. "Suicide Prevention: The Significance of the Semicolon." *A Second Chance, Inc.*, www.asecondchance-kinship.com/suicide-prevention-the-significance-of-the-semicolon/. Accessed 26 Oct. 2024.

Resilience

1. *Leave No Trace*. Directed by Debra Granik, performances by Ben Foster and Thomasin McKenzie, Bleecker Street, 2018.

Toll For Thee

1. Donne, John. *Devotions upon Emergent Occasions and Death's Duel.* Vintage Books, 1999, p. 108.

Grief as Negation

1. Rogers, C. H., Floyd, F. J., Seltzer, M. M., Greenberg, J., & Hong, J. (2008). "Long-term effects of the death of a child on parents' adjustment in midlife." *Journal of Family Psychology,* 22(2), pp. 203-211, https://doi.org/10.1037/0893-3200.22.2.203

Grief Fingerprint

1. Van der Kolk, Bessel A. *The Body Keeps the Score: Brain, Mind, and Body in the Healing of Trauma.* Penguin Books, 2015.
2. Bereaved mother of John Paul Raphael, Elizabeth Leon, shared some helpful insights in a comment on my blog. She suggested looking into Worden's Tasks of Mourning or the dual-process model as more descriptive frameworks for understanding child loss over long periods of time.

   Reference: Leon, Elizabeth. Personal communication. Comment on *Endure.* 21, May, 2024, https://endure.blog

How Ought a Man to Grieve the Loss of His Child?

1. This chapter originally appeared as an article in *We Need Not Walk Alone,* the national magazine of The Compassionate Friends, an organization offering support to families grieving the death of a child. The magazine features stories and articles written by and for parents, siblings, and grandparents navigating the grief journey.

   You can read the full article in the Spring 2024 issue of *We Need Not Walk Alone,* pages 8-9, available here.

   A heartfelt thank you to *The Compassionate Friends* for the opportunity to share my story and to Cathy Seehuetter for her invaluable editing support.

EI

1. Berger, Ron. *An Ethic of Excellence: Building a Culture of Craftsmanship with Students*. Heinemann, 2003.
2. Crandall, Brian. *Montana Fire Service Training School*. Montana State University

Thinking of You, Cooper Spotify Playlist

1. A curated playlist titled "Thinking of you, Cooper" was created as part of my healing process. This playlist is available on Spotify and can be accessed here: Thinking of you, Cooper. https://open.spotify.com/playlist/6QtOVq5DKO7LHPapnM06yw?si= 6a0a325d251741cb

Surfers, Mosaic Artists, and Carpenters

1. *100 Foot Wave*. Directed by Chris Smith, produced by Joe Lewis, Maria Zuckerman, Ryan Heller, and Michael Bloom, HBO, 2021.

Just to Be With You

1. Scott, Calum. "You Are the Reason." *Only Human*, Capitol Records, 2018.

Appendix B

1. Masten, Ann S. *Ordinary Magic: Resilience in Development*. Guilford Press, 2014.
2. Masten, Ann S. *Ordinary Magic: Resilience in Development*. Guilford Press, 2014.
3. Ungar, Michael. *The Social Ecology of Resilience: A Handbook of Theory and Practice*. Springer, 2012.

appendix a
Outline of Cooper's Funeral Service

October 20, 2023

Funeral Service delivered by Kelly McCoy, Cooper's father

Background song looped - "Forrest Gump Suite" by Alan Silvestri

Welcome/Thank You

(Turn music off)

Welcome, family and friends, as we pay our final tribute of love and respect to Cooper James and lay his body to rest next to his grandfather and great-grandparents. The Lord be with you.

The order of service today will be as follows:

- Invocation
- Prayers for the family (anointing)
- Prayers for Cooper
- Readings: Old Testament, New Testament, Gospel, and poems
- Eulogy: Remembering Cooper
- The Lord's Prayer

- Blessing the grave
- Commending Cooper to the Lord
- Final prayers

Please turn off cell phones, including vibration.

Tears and crying are okay. Take deep breaths—in through the nose, slowly, deeply, and completely. Hold it briefly, then let it out slowly, deeply, and completely.

Invocation

We call upon God to gather and be here with us.

In the name of the Father, Son, and Holy Spirit.

Lord, Holy Spirit, giver of life, be here with us today. We praise and bless You for Your mercy and kindness. You alone are our refuge and strength. You sanctify the homes of the living and make holy the places of the dead. You alone open the gates and lead us into the mansions of the saints.

Almighty and ever-living God, remember the mercy with which You graced Your beloved son Cooper James in this life. Receive him, we pray, into the mansions of the saints. As You bless this resting place, look also with favor on those who mourn, and comfort them in their loss. Amen.

Prayer for the Family

Lord, You have taught us to strengthen the bonds of family through faith, honor, and love. Look kindly upon parents Victoria and Kelly, who sought to bind their child to You. Look kindly upon Cooper's siblings, CJ, Carse, and Grace. Look kindly upon Cooper's grandparents, Lois, Kathy, and James. Look kindly upon Uncle Jason, Aunt Shell, and cousin Ry. Look kindly upon Cooper's dog, Snoopy, and also Bear Bear and Willow. Look kindly upon Cooper's precious friends, especially

Ethan, Johnathan, Jacob, Chase, and Abby. Lord, bring us one day to Your heavenly home, where the saints dwell in blessedness and peace. Amen.

Anointing of the Family for Healing

(Anointing oil - frankincense, rosemary, cinnamon)

[Song - "Canon in D" by Chamberlain Brass 1:28]

Prayers for Cooper

Lord, whose mercies cannot be numbered, accept our prayers on behalf of Your beloved son, Cooper James, and welcome him into the land of light and joy, the land of peace, eternal happiness, and health, that he may now enjoy infinite fellowship with You and those who have gone before him.

Lord, grant Cooper James perfect rest beneath the sheltering wings of Your presence. We pray he may be among the holy and pure, who shine with brightness in the heavens.

Lord, may Cooper's repose be in paradise. Lord of mercy, bring him under the cover of Your wings forever, and bind his soul in the bond of eternal life. Lord, be Cooper's possession, and grant that he may forever rest in peace.

We ask this in the name of the Father, Son, and Holy Spirit. Amen.

Readings

In the Rising Sun, Adapted (Poem)

> In the rising of the sun and in its going down, remember
> him;
> In the blowing of the wind and in the chill of winter,
> remember him;

In the opening of buds and in the rebirth of spring,
remember him;
In the rustling of leaves and in the beauty of autumn,
remember him;
In the beginning of the year and when it ends, remember
him;
When we are weary and in need of strength, remember
him;
When we are lost and sick at heart, remember him;
When we have joys we yearn to share, remember him.
So long as we live, he too shall live, for he is a part of us as
we remember him.

Psalm 23 (Old Testament)

The Lord is my shepherd; I shall not want.
He makes me to lie down in green pastures;
He leads me beside the still waters.
He restores my soul;
He leads me in the paths of righteousness for His name's
sake.
Yea, though I walk through the valley of the shadow of
death, I will fear no evil; for You are with me; Your rod
and Your staff, they comfort me.
You prepare a table before me in the presence of my
enemies; You anoint my head with oil; my cup runs
over.
Surely goodness and mercy shall follow me all the days of
my life; and I will dwell in the house of the Lord forever.

Romans 8:31, Adapted (New Testament)

Brothers and sisters:

If God is for us, who can be against us?

What will separate us from the love of Christ?

Will anguish, or distress, or persecution, or famine, or nakedness, or peril, or the sword?

No, in all these things, we conquer overwhelmingly through Him who loved us.

For I am convinced that neither death, nor life, nor angels, nor principalities, nor present things, nor future things, nor powers, nor height, nor depth, nor any other creature will be able to separate us from the love of God in Christ Jesus our Lord.

Matthew 11 (Gospel) – Jesus Speaking

"Come to me, all you who are weary and burdened, and I will give you rest. Take my yoke upon you and learn from me, for I am gentle and humble in heart, and you will find rest for your souls. For my yoke is easy, and my burden is light."

Silence/Remembering Cooper Together, a Quaker Tradition

Eulogy, Stories

Cooper was funny, intelligent, gentle, good-natured, and a good soul. Cooper was loved by all and was easy to be around. Cooper loved animals, and he loved soccer. He was an Aerospace engineer, a pilot, a creator of new words—he pegged "ginormous" long before it was a word. Cooper was the kind of person who preferred a few close friendships.

- Learning to swim, him on my back, arms around my neck.
- Snoopy, Rowdy, the night he got him. "That's the one, Dad." "I know."
- Cooper was to be valedictorian and read puns. He graduated #4 in his class.

Pallbearers: Kelly, Pat, CJ, Carse. Placing of the casket above gravesite.

Prayer of Blessing for the Grave

(Holy water, blessing the casket and gravesite in the name of the Father, the Son, and the Holy Spirit.)

Three shrouds of linen placed over the casket by CJ, Carse, and Grace, each with a blessed beeswax candle on top.

Lord, by whose mercy the faithful departed find their rest, bless this grave, and send Your holy angels to watch over it. As we bury here the body of Cooper James, deliver his soul from every bond of sin, that he may rejoice in You with Your saints forever and ever. Amen.

In the name of the Father, Son, and Holy Spirit, we commit Cooper James' body to this holy and sacred ground: earth to earth, ashes to ashes, and dust to dust. Amen.

The Lord's Prayer

All family and friends form a circle around the casket, holding hands, and pray the Lord's Prayer together. Afterward, pass around a wooden bowl of dirt for each to place a handful on top of the casket.

[Song - "You Are Mine" by David Haas]

Commend to the Lord

Lord, in the sure and certain hope of the resurrection to eternal life through You, we commend to You Your beloved son Cooper James, who was reborn by water and the Holy Spirit in Baptism. Receive him into the arms of Your mercy, into the blessed rest of everlasting peace, and into the glorious company of the saints in light.

Lord, bless him and keep him, shine Your face upon him and be gracious to him, lift up Your countenance upon him, and give him peace. Amen.

[Song - "Memorial" by Ike Ndolo]

Final Prayers

Lowering of the casket into the grave.

Lord, from the deep places beyond words, thank You for Cooper James and the special way in which he touched each of our lives.

Lord, now, with trembling in our bodies but confidence in You, we completely turn Cooper James over to You and ask that You hold Cooper's hand for eternity. Pull him close to Your chest, Lord, hold him tight, and love him. Grant him love, peace, and eternal happiness.

Listen, Lord, to the prayers of Your servants on behalf of Cooper James, and grant to him, whose funeral we have celebrated today, the inheritance promised to all Your saints.

Lord, we pray that You would watch over each and every one of us here today, guiding and protecting us, offering us safety, health, and happiness for our journeys. May we, too, strive to live a life of kindness and gentleness as we have watched Cooper do so in his life.

In the name of the Father, Son, and Holy Spirit. Amen.

appendix b
Practical Resilience

Losing a child, sibling, or grandchild is one of the most difficult adversities a person can experience in life. It's easily at the top of the list.

What may help to achieve a resilient outcome?

Let's start with a brief history of resilience.

Researchers during World War II studied negative outcomes. (Even today, Western medicine is largely "disease-based," focusing on what's wrong rather than what's right.)

However, a small group of researchers became interested in those who faced great adversity yet thrived despite formidable odds. These researchers began asking different questions: Who endures adversity and recovers well, and why? Could these lessons be applied to help others?[1]

Thus, resilience science was born.

This means that the study of resilience focuses on strengths, not deficits.

When it comes to grief and child loss, the question becomes: What is going right? We already know there is a lot going wrong, but even if it's minuscule, what is going right? What strengths can I build on?

For example, in the early days after Cooper's death, I noticed that I was still showering, brushing my teeth, drinking coffee in the morning, walking the dogs, and making a list of three things to do each day. I was also writing. These might not seem monumental, but they were early strengths I could build from.

Find your strengths and "grow edges" from them.

As a retired firefighter, I worked in a very "manly" culture. In such cultures, there is a pervasive myth that all an individual needs to "bounce back" after adversity is personal grit. Resilience, in these settings—and in popular understanding—is often steeped in the myth that recovering and adapting after adversity is purely an internal characteristic.

This is not true.

The reality, supported by cross-cultural studies in resilience over time, is that resilience is more about resources and relationships —access to supports—than about personal grit. This is why Dr. Ann S. Masten calls resilience "ordinary magic."

What may help us survive and thrive after child or sibling loss is access to resources that support us: counseling, support groups, doctor visits, time in nature, faith-wisdom communities, and more.

In times of significant adversity, it is Tribe that matters, not individualism. This is the story of resilience.

I encourage those experiencing significant loss to lean into family and friends, accepting the grace of support.

After years of studying this topic, I have my own brief definition of resilience: *Resilience = Relationships, Resources, Ruggedness, Reserves, Rest & Recovery.*

Here are some established definitions of resilience:

> *The capacity of a dynamic system to adapt successfully to disturbances that threaten system function, viability, or development.*[2] — Dr. Ann S. Masten, University of Minnesota

> *In the presence of significant adversity, resilience is the capacity of individuals to navigate their way to resources that sustain their well-being, and their capacity to individually and collectively negotiate for these resources to be provided in culturally meaningful ways.*[3] — Dr. Michael Ungar, Dalhousie University

Notice that Dr. Masten focuses on "systems" and Dr. Ungar emphasizes navigating and negotiating for resources.

There's much to consider in resilience science beyond this appendix, but let me leave you with this:

Make resilient moves.

Even if they are micro-moves, take small, resilient steps each day to help rebuild your new self. There is no timeline, and there is no single "right" path to resilience (whether it's recovery, adaptation, transformation, or any combination of these).

Here are some resilient moves you can make that may help (feel free to create your own):

- Spend time with family and friends. Lean into relationships that support and uplift you.
- If you need to go pro, go pro. There is no shame in seeing a counselor. In fact, you probably should.
- Seek peer support from those you trust.

- Spend time with your pets.
- Set a few small goals.
- Spend time in nature.
- Exercise is healing—even slow walks.
- Don't forget to rest.
- Eat healthy foods—reds, blues, and greens.
- Be willing to learn and grow.
- Get out and have a few beers with friends (in moderation).
- Garden.
- Cook or bake.
- Talk to a mentor or coach.
- Learn to meditate and practice mindfulness.
- Practice breathing exercises.
- Visualize yourself doing well—positive visualization.
- Share your story with others.
- Speak with your faith-wisdom leader.
- Debrief what has happened—talk it out.
- Take breaks when you need them.
- Socialize lightly.
- Develop calming self-talk: "I am strong and resilient."
- Remember to laugh again, eventually.
- Go to the doctor.
- Get in the water—the research is clear, water is healing.
- Attend religious services.
- Take a mental health day if you need it. You come first.
- Adopt a growth mindset: "I'm not feeling great today, but I'll feel better tomorrow."
- Lean into your hobbies, or develop new ones.
- Write or journal—writing has been very healing for me.
- Pray.
- Take a class—education and learning can help.
- Read a book.

- Establish a routine—routine has been important in my healing process.
- Focus on sleep architecture and hygiene—sleep is crucial for recovery.

Remember, your grief isn't likely to go away. What is happening is that your ability to sit with and lean into grief is growing stronger. The grief will always be there, but you are growing stronger.

Your life has been devastated, and I understand. I know. You won't be "okay," but you will be okay.

You're going to make it. Even if it's tattered and messy, form an outline of a life to live for—a rugged hope for the future. We now have a commitment to live this life the best we can, to honor the child, sibling, or grandchild we've lost.

appendix c
Thinking of You, Cooper Spotify Playlist

1. *Weight Of Your World. Higher,* by Chris Stapleton, Mercury Nashville, 2023.

2. *Home. The World From The Side Of The Moon,* by Phillip Phillips, 19 Recordings/Interscope, 2012.

3. *I'll Be Missing You (feat. Faith Evans, 112). Bad Boy's 10th Anniversary: The Hits,* by Diddy, Faith Evans, and 112, Bad Boy Records, 2004.

4. *Til It Happens To You. Til It Happens To You,* by Lady Gaga, Interscope, 2015.

5. *Mountains Of My Mind. Higher,* by Chris Stapleton, Mercury Nashville, 2023.

6. *Not Right Now. Love Will Have The Final Word,* by Jason Gray, Centricity Music, 2014.

7. *Rescue. Look Up Child,* by Lauren Daigle, Centricity Music/Warner Records, 2018.

8. *Bruises. Divinely Uninspired To A Hellish Extent,* by Lewis Capaldi, Vertigo Berlin, 2019.

9. *Dreaming with a Broken Heart. Continuum*, by John Mayer, Aware/Columbia, 2006.

10. *Stairway to Heaven - Remaster. Led Zeppelin IV (Deluxe Edition)*, by Led Zeppelin, Atlantic Records, 1971.

11. *Lost Boy. Lost Boy*, by Ruth B., Columbia, 2015.

12. *Just Breathe. Backspacer*, by Pearl Jam, Monkeywrench Records, 2009.

13. *To Be A Man (feat. Darius Rucker). To Be A Man*, by Dax and Darius Rucker, Records/Columbia, 2023.

14. *Tha Crossroads. E. 1999 Eternal*, by Bone Thugs-N-Harmony, Ruthless Records, 1995.

15. *The Winner Is. Little Miss Sunshine (Original Motion Picture Soundtrack)*, by DeVotchKa and Mychael Danna, Lakeshore Records, 2006.

16. *Someone You Loved. Divinely Uninspired To A Hellish Extent*, by Lewis Capaldi, Vertigo Berlin, 2019.

17. *Nothing Compares 2 U. I Do Not Want What I Haven't Got*, by Sinéad O'Connor, Chrysalis Records, 1990.

18. *Saturn. Atlas: I*, by Sleeping At Last, Asteroid B-612, 2014.

19. *Free Falling. 35 Acoustic Pop Hits*, by Guitar Tribute Players, CC Entertainment, 2012.

20. *He Ain't Heavy, He's My Brother. Super Hits*, by The Hollies, Epic/Legacy, 1967.

21. *Cat's in the Cradle. Verities & Balderdash*, by Harry Chapin, Rhino/Elektra, 1974.

22. *Go Rest High On That Mountain. When Love Finds You*, by Vince Gill, Geffen, 1994.

23. *Broken Halos. From A Room: Volume 1,* by Chris Stapleton, Mercury Nashville, 2017.

24. *Stone. Feel Something,* by Jaymes Young, Atlantic Records, 2017.

25. *Burden. The Wild Swan,* by Foy Vance, Gingerbread Man Records/Elektra, 2016.

26. *Ball and Chain. Social Distortion,* by Social Distortion, Epic, 1990.

27. *Sweet Child O' Mine. Appetite For Destruction,* by Guns N' Roses, Guns N Roses P&D, 1987.

28. *Weight Of The World. The Human Condition,* by Jon Bellion, Blaque Keyz, Capitol Records, 2016.

29. *Youth of the Nation. Satellite,* by P.O.D., Atlantic Records, 2001.

30. *1-800-273-8255. Everybody,* by Logic, Alessia Cara, and Khalid, Def Jam Recordings, 2017.

31. *Fade To Black. Ride The Lightning,* by Metallica, Blackened Recordings, 1984.

32. *Nothing Compares 2 U - Live At SiriusXM/2015. Chris Cornell (Deluxe Edition),* by Chris Cornell, A&M, 2018.

33. *Daydream. Daydream,* by Lily Meola, Nettwerk Music Group, 2021.

34. *Beautiful. Stripped,* by Christina Aguilera, RCA Records, 2002.

35. *I Won't Give Up. Love Is a Four Letter Word (Deluxe Edition),* by Jason Mraz, Atlantic Records, 2012.

36. *Unsteady. VHS,* by X Ambassadors, Kid Ina Korner / Interscope, 2015.

37. *I Am Not Okay. I Am Not Okay*, by Jelly Roll, BBR Music Group/Jelly Roll, 2024.

38. *The Sound of Silence. Immortalized*, by Disturbed, Reprise, 2015.

39. *Everybody Hurts. Automatic For The People*, by R.E.M., Concord Records, 1992.

40. *Memorial. Memorial*, by Ike Ndolo, Ike Ndolo, 2015.

41. *Dancing in the Sky. Million Eyes*, by Sam Barber, Lockeland Springs/Atlantic, 2023.

42. *Dancing in the Sky. Dancing in the Sky*, by Dani and Lizzy, 604 Records, 2015.

43. *Leaving - 2017 Remaster. Elysium: Further Listening 2011 - 2012 (2017 Remaster)*, by Pet Shop Boys, Rhino, 2012.

44. *Rainbow. Golden Hour*, by Kacey Musgraves, MCA Nashville, 2018.

45. *Father And Son - Remastered 2020. Tea For The Tillerman (Super Deluxe)*, by Yusuf / Cat Stevens, UMC (Universal Music Catalogue), 2020.

46. *The Father, My Son, And The Holy Ghost. God, Family, Country (Deluxe Edition)*, by Craig Morgan, Broken Bow Records, 2020.

47. *The Gospel is Rest. The Gospel is Rest*, by Elias Dummer and Land of Color, Integrity Music, 2021.

48. *I Will Carry You. Canyon*, by Ellie Holcomb, Ellie Holcomb, 2021.

49. *In the End. Hybrid Theory (Bonus Edition)*, by Linkin Park, Warner Records, 2000.

50. *My Hero. The Colour And The Shape*, by Foo Fighters, RCA Records Label, 1997.

51. *High Tide Or Low Tide. Mix: Reggae and Ska*, by Ben Harper and Jack Johnson, UME - Global Clearing House, 2024.

52. *You Are The Reason. Only Human (Deluxe)*, by Calum Scott, Capitol Records, 2018.

Scan the QR Code to visit the playlist:

about the author

Kelly is a husband, father, dog dad, and author living in the Midwest. He frequently teaches and gives public presentations on resilience, grief, and personal growth.

Kelly is an educator, former director of fire training, former faculty member and academic senator at the university, and retired fire department division chief. Kelly left the fire department in 2015 after a 25-year career, transitioning to work in higher education.

Kelly received undergraduate and graduate degrees in liberal studies and education, later completing graduate work in philosophy and theology.

Kelly has studied resilience through the University of Oklahoma, University of Minnesota, Dalhousie University, 02X Human Performance, and training abroad.

Kelly enjoys being in the mountains, dogs, sun on his face, crisp, cold air, being outdoors, drinking local craft beer, reading books, and spending time with family and friends.

X x.com/elephantsecho
 instagram.com/elephantsecho